AF574968

by James Alinder

Untitled 18
The Friends of Photography

CUMMING
PHOTOGRAPHS

Acknowledgements

Having been enthusiastic about Robert Cumming's photographs for the past decade, it was a particular pleasure to produce this book. I am grateful to Robert Cumming for his complete cooperation with this project, for providing a retrospective selection of his photographs and for participating in a detailed interview. The photographs reproduced here were selected from work exhibited in our gallery February 23 to March 23, 1979. It is exciting for me to bring this work, which I greatly enjoy, to a larger audience.

I would also like to thank my staff for their assistance during the project. Thanks to David Featherstone for editorial thoroughness, to Peter Andersen for skillfully supervising the printing production and to Nancy Ponedel, who served as my secretary. The helpful comments of Mary Alinder, Robert Baker and Andrea Turnage are also greatly appreciated.

In addition, thanks are due to the National Endowment for the Arts for their support in publishing this book.

J.A.

Colophon

Type: Megaron light
Paper: Flokote, 100 lb.
Typography: Instant Type, Monterey, California
Printing: Herald Printers, Monterey, California
Binding: Cardoza-James Binding, San Francisco
Press run: 3500 copies

The Friends of Photography

The Friends of Photography, founded in 1967, is a not-for-profit organization actively involved in the support and encouragement of creative photography. The programs of The Friends include publications, grants to photographers, exhibitions, workshops, lectures and critical inquiry. The publications of The Friends of Photography are devoted to the presentation of contemporary photographers' work as well as to the history and criticism of the medium. Membership is open to everyone. Inquiries should be addressed to The Friends of Photography, P.O. Box 239, Carmel, California 93921.

Untitled 18

This publication is the eighteenth in a series of publications on serious photography by The Friends of Photography. Some previous issues are still available.

ISSN 0163-7916
ISBN #0-933286-09-0
Library of Congress Catalogue Card No. 78-75261
$6.95

THE PHOTOGRAPHS OF ROBERT CUMMING

The current generation of photographers seems more concerned with the ideas which a picture presents than with the discovery and interpretation of subject matter from the visual world. While images made specifically to interpret ideas have occurred in the history of photography, they have been outside the mainstream. Photographers have traditionally accepted the boundaries of the visual world as the limits of photography, without extending their search further to the limits of their imagination. For over a century people, places and things were the natural subject matter for photography. Many photographers have come to feel that this material has been exhausted.

Creative people are not interested in making photographs similar to what thousands of other photographers have done and thus have either attemped to refine nuances of traditional concerns or have looked in completely different directions. One of the directions they have taken over the past decade has been to explore the "process". This has been seen in the rebirth of older processes such as gum bichromate and cyanotype. Other interests include work in mixed media and the aggressive investigation of new technology. A direction of particular interest, and one which shows possibilities for continued growth, is the photographic presentation of abstract ideas, a development which has paralleled the increased use of photography by conceptual artists.

Even though it had been an undercurrent for decades, conceptual art emerged as a formal art movement in the 1960's as an extreme response of the dictum "less is more". The philosophical roots of the movement lie in the belief that ideas are the most important human product; presentation through an actual art object is secondary. Taken to its logical extreme, this theory implies that art ultimately has no physical object.

While a few visual artists found the idea of art without objects appealing in its pure form, most felt the need for a vehicle to share their ideas with an audience. Photography was often the medium selected for that sharing because of its utility in the documentation of ideas. It thus entered at the core of the conceptual movement. Of the several artists who refined their use of photography while maintaining a distinctly conceptual approach, Robert Cumming is one of the most important.

As a child, Cumming was a self-taught and compulsive artist. His formal art education, which included both bachelor's and master's degrees, initially focused on drawing and painting, but later on sculpture and, finally, photography. While his primary statement over the past few years has been in photography, he continues to work actively in other media. In fact, he calls on his skills as a sculptor to construct the basic "subject matter" for many of his photographs. For most photographers the object to be photographed is raw material. For Cumming, the objects which he constructs to be used in his photographs are an inherent part of the creative process as well as subjects.

The photographs reproduced in this book trace the evolution of Cumming's photography chronologically over the past decade. Observed broadly, they seem particularly uniform. Yet on closer inspection both continuity and change are apparent. The change is not always clear, however, because Cumming often returns to earlier themes. His themes include interruptions in landscape and logic (the title he gave to his most recent book), reappraisal of everyday objects, debunking of the polished presentation of art photographs, ironic and absurd reversals of the expected, distorted time relationships, reconsideration of form and function, out-and-out illusionism and magic tricks, satires on the misreading of natural phenomena and sardonic commentaries on the history of art and photography. To present these ideas as photographs, the objects placed in front of the camera have been purposefully directed; Cumming has carefully constructed and arranged them to provide the visual expression of his concept. In the pages which follow, I will emphasize Cumming's themes while discussing several of his photographs.

The first photograph, *Watermelon/Bread, 1970* (plate 1), is, I believe, a masterpiece which addressed many of the questions and helped set the tone for conceptual photography during the 1970's. I found it amazing, meaningful, mysterious and delightful when I first saw it in 1971 and still do today. It is a fully realized concept utilizing commonly found objects and the purely photographic resources of the 8x10 contact print. We too often see "one time" photographs, images with visual, emotional and intellectual interest so slight that it is depleted after one viewing. *Watermelon/Bread* is one of the many Cumming photographs which lasts. Cumming selected it for the cover of his first book, *Picture Fictions,* published in 1971.

As subject matter for his visualized concept, Cumming has used the common artistic genre of the still life, but it is clear that his photograph is a pastiche. We are immediately drawn to the ironic central object — the piece of bread grafted to the side of the watermelon — by its location, tonality, focus, and above all, its unexpected content. The watermelon itself has been cut to half its original length and has been cut at a slight angle so that we can see its widest diameter.

This central figure of the still life was constructed on an ordinary kitchen table, a table cluttered with the common litter of life — a postcard, a pepper mill, a box of extra-strength something. Nearly all of the objects in the photograph, both organic and inorganic, are round. The focus is soft everywhere except on the transplanted bread. The subsidiary items in the photograph seem not to have been specifically chosen or positioned within the frame, but are as random as the watermelon is precise.

On one level *Watermelon/Bread* is concerned with the idea of grafting, and suggests that mother nature will take revenge when we know no better than to mix completely natural ingredients with those refined by industry. Socio-political comments such as this can easily be inferred from Cumming's photographs, but I do not feel that his intention is to push the ideas this far. Since we can never fully know the intentions of the artist, however, understanding and appreciation must come from ourselves. Cumming's photographs may be "read" as fully as you wish, but they often need to be confronted for an extended period of time since many of them will not give up their secrets easily.

120 Alternatives (from an original edition of 1000) (plate 2) presents a couch scattered with sheets of printed paper. The imprint tells you what the image is about; each sheet reads, "Plurally or in a pile we are sculpture, singularly I am a print". In part, Cumming's statement regards the potential of a two dimensional object to gain the third dimension and also comments on our compulsion to make categories. After we accept the statement on the sheets of paper, we next come to realize that we are not even looking at a sculpture or a lithograph, but at a photograph. And the photograph is a separate statement, an object unto itself.

Cumming's photograph of the Coleman cooler in the desert (plate 3) presents us with utterly conflicting realities. Normally we are enthralled by nature; wilderness is to be revered, protected and saved. Plastic is the antithesis. In Cumming's photograph our feelings about the two are reversed. Nature is seen as inhospitable, the desert plants are exploding forms ready to violate our space, with a rattler or scorpion hiding behind each one. Plastic, however, is controlled, reassuring and lifesaving. Is this the new truth, a mirage, or an invitation to a picnic on the stage set at Universal Studios?

Between 1973 and 1977 most of Cumming's photographs were done as multiple-print pieces, usually with two 8x10 contact prints mounted side-by-side on a large mat. Characteristically there is a carefully developed narrative relationship between the two prints. *Blast Sequence* (plates 4-7), the first sequential image reproduced, is unusual in having four images. It is also the first of several commentaries on the medium of photography itself. The reference here is to the amazing ability of photography to arrest action, and to Dr. Harold Edgerton's microsecond bullet-stopping strobe photographs. John Szarkowski, commenting on Edgerton's images in *Looking at Photographs,* wrote of the " . . . exposure of extremely short duration, so short that it seemed to show empty spaces between the thinnest slices of time". In *Blast Sequence* Cumming has separated and arrested those thinnest slices of time. We realize that the photographer has carefully constructed this four-part instant replay. With the floodlight illuminating the subject, his exposures were about 30 seconds long. This animation suspended in time is a theme which Cumming returns to several times, shown here in plates 16 & 17, 20 & 21, 22 & 23 and 32 & 33.

Another central theme in *Blast Sequence* is Cumming's desire to remind us that we are looking at a photograph; he wants his hand to show. This sequence includes the floodlights, the source of illumination of the photograph, within the frame. Cumming usually leaves more around the edges of the subject than we expect; he does not fill the frame with the central subject, but allows us to see its context. In *Blast Sequence* the floodlights also burn out the upper part of the palm trees. Graphically these two lighter areas and the main subject create a triangle which strengthens the composition. This theme is repeated in plates 10 & 11, 12, 20 & 21, 36 and 37.

At times Cumming derives idea referents from sources outside his own observation and thoughts. A friend once mentioned to him a scene in a film in which Ansel Adams is shown working on a commercial assignment, making a photograph for a dried fruit company advertising their raisins in a professional bakery magazine. Not satisfied with the way regular raisin bread looked, the advertising people carefully hollowed out pockets in the sandwich bread and painstakingly placed raisins in the bread so that it would be seen as perfect by Adams' camera. In the raisin bread pair (plates 10 & 11) Cumming presents his conceptual representation of the situation. Obviously there was as much sleight of hand involved in that Adams photograph as there is in the work of Robert Cumming.

While the raisin bread anecdote provides the title for the photographs, Cumming uses it as a foil to present his other concerns. In this instance they include conflict between expected environments, altered perspectives and a contrast between natural and artificial surfaces. The set for the advertising photograph has been moved out of the studio and restaged outdoors and at night. Not only have the table legs been sawed off, but the front legs are even shorter than the back to provide an altered perspective showing the whole table-top. The lush foliage of the natural background is a harsh contrast to the brick contact paper which forms the artificial floor.

Robert Cumming refers to the quirks of his mind as another major source for his conceptualizations. These quirks are certainly visable in the highly absurd *Mosquito Field* (plate 13). Imagine a gaggle of mosquitos evenly spaced on a field. Conceptually the presentation is a comment on formalism in recent painting. A more direct meaning is elicited by all those who have had frequent and unfortunate contact with mosquitos. The 100 mosquitos constructed and photographed by Cumming initially appear to be alive. Singly they are more a nuisance than a threat, but 100 could be menacing.

The relationship between the amount of time spent conceptualizing, constructing and photographing in Cumming's work is radically different from what we commonly expect in photography. Of course the percentages vary with each piece, but Cumming spends perhaps an average of 45% of his time thinking, 45% building the subject — the 100 mosquitos, for example — and 10% actually making the picture.

The pair *Of 8 Balls Dropped off the Peak of the Roof, 2 Fell on the North Side, 6 Favored the East* (plates 16 & 17) are classic Cumming photographs. The props are visually less complex than those in many of the pairs, but the concept is refreshing and the results wonderful. For me, the major reference in these photographs is to a scientific attitude. We are becoming increasingly statistically oriented, but must we always care about the data? Do we expect Cumming's caption to tell us how many times the balls were dropped? Whether this is the "median" or "mean" or just the result of a one-time drop? Close observation reveals that the photograph on the left side is the mirror image of the other, and that the two balls on the north are in exactly the same location on the east, with four balls added. Never trust raw data.

Of 8 balls dropped . . . , is also one of Cumming's most graphic pieces. By his flipping of the negative, Cumming has created the corner of the "building", a visual right angle of the north and east sides which changes our perception of the space. Compositionally the pair of prints is beautifully welded. Further graphic interest is found in the contrast of both color and shape between the dark slats of the building, with their subtle yet strong horizontal lines, and the round white balls.

This piece, like *Blast Sequence,* and the other "freeze frame" photographs, is closely allied to the theme of Cumming as a magician. Despite a long standing public notion that photographs tell the truth, that they can and should be believed, there is abundant evidence that all photographs are replete with lies and fabrications. At the very most they give us a modest monocular appearance of one aspect of a subject. Amazingly, we routinely expect approximate truth from still photographs, and we are nonplussed when confronted with sleight of hand. For Cumming, illusionism and artifice are fundamental, and as with the magician, we are advised not to pose technical questions, but simply to enjoy.

Too often conceptual art is excrutiatingly intellectual. Robert Cumming modifies this intellectual quality with wit and a pictorial concern, as seen in *Fast and Slow Rain — Driving Rain and Downpour* (plates 20 & 21). The spring shower and the driving rain of a thunderstorm are visually contrasted in a highly stylized treatment; the rain-prop is constructed in the style of a cartoon. Cumming provides a symbolic representation which places his photograph somewhere in the gap between a cartoon and reality.

Again Cumming allows his hand to show as he lets us see the wooden frame holding the partially painted pieces of white string. The strong linear structure of these prints is a repeated device which will be used again in *Leaning Structures* (plates 30 & 31) and in the Universal Studio stills (plates 36 & 37).

The photographs titled *Cross-body, Pen-Point Choreography* (plates 24-27) are Cumming's first use in this book of human figures. In fact, they are self-portraits and refer to Cumming's role as a writer. In several of his books, his text takes more space than his photographs and is intended as an integral part of the total statement. Another rationale for the pen-point group is Cumming's life-long admiration of penmanship and graphology.

The vastly oversized pen-points remind me of the dance-routine props of Busby Berkeley films. One of the more refreshing aspects of Cumming's prop-building is his free investigation of scale and content as he makes the transition from gigantic pen-points to microscopic mosquitos, from realistic buildings to surrealistic shoes. There is in these props an emphasis on authenticity and craft and a decided concern with details.

Leaning Structures (plates 30 & 31), another reference to art history, has a certain relationship with DaVinci drawings, but it is also an echo of Cumming's earlier concerns with the figure and with architectural engineering. In several of these previous pieces Cumming created lines by stretching string on and around the model. Here the lines are drawn on the surface of the photograph. In the structural configuration of this pair of photographs most of the weight of the subjects is transferred through the arms to the wall. The engineering of the stresses might be similar to that encountered in the design of flying buttresses.

As light exposes film, *Energy Transforms Matter* (plates 34 & 35). This pair of photographs again works on many levels and is certainly one of the most memorable sequences in the book. The print on the left is the conceptual quintessence of the contemporary industrial photograph, with welding sparks forming perfect arcs on the film. The print on the right has the superficial character of a supermarket meat advertisement.

There is often, in Cumming's conceptualizations, a tension between the form of an object and its function. In *Energy Transforms Matter* this relationship is less arcane. In most of the photographs I have discussed it has been Cumming's energy as a sculptor which has transformed various matter into the nominal subjects for his photographs. Here, wire rods are being joined by the energy of 6000-degree heat to make a grate which has the potential function of a barbeque. Finally something eminently practical, I hear his mother saying, has come of the sculpture. However, as Cumming would have it, all the available energy was used to weld the grid and none is left to grill the steaks.

Plates 36 & 37 are not paired photographs, but were both made at the Universal Studio movie-production stages. The idea of Robert Cumming, who has often utilized the "special effects" of the movie industry, actually photographing the studio's props on their sets is most appealing. With the Hollywood props as ready-made found objects, and conceptually viable props at that, Cumming goes right to work. Some of the results of this effort were included in the 1978 portfolio Cumming produced called *Studio Still Lifes*.

As in his other "documentations", Cumming allows us, in these photographs, to understand the basis of the illusions which Hollywood makes by including the subject of the film-scene as well as the surrounding mechanism or set. The two selections reproduced here demonstrate Cumming's interest in the geometric aspects of the studio. Again, the multiplicity of lines appear. Photographic composition has never seemed as important for Cumming as it does in these two prints. The sense of scale here is also considerably different from that of his other work since he has included the vast interior spaces of the studios.

The final photograph in the book, made only a few months ago, is indicative of Cumming's return to the single photograph as a statement. However, in *Quick Shift of the Head Leaves Glowing Stool Afterimage Posited on Pedestal* (plate 39) we see the photograph is, in fact, split in half. Cumming has drawn a vertical line where the background changes tone, dividing the photograph as though he cannot quite let go of the paired-photograph concept.

The event photographed here does actually occur. The stool stands in a very strong beam of light which burns its outline into the retina of the eye. As the eyes move quickly to the pedestal in shadow, the image of the stool appears with natural magic. In Cumming's visualization, its color is reversed and the strong shadows have disappeared from around the stool, replaced by the glow which surrounds the afterimage. The reference here can be extended to psychological tests and games and to Op Art and color-field painting.

The captions which accompany Cumming's photographs are sometimes merely labels, yet often they are vital links to understanding. While drawing on the narrative abilities of the photograph, especially in the paired images, Cumming uses the captions to spark our interpretation. He points out connections which the viewer may not have been able to determine from the photographs alone. However, Cumming has also been known to add a caption which leads nowhere.

While most conceptual artists use photography merely as a tool to document their ideas, Cumming is concerned with the medium of photography itself. These photographs, with their environmental backgrounds, are considerably more interesting as pictures than are typical conceptual documents. Cumming has also chosen the 8x10 view camera as the instrument for his picture making. He selected the format for its ability to resolve detail, but he does not place emphasis on other potential advantages of the large negative. It would seem too fussy for him to be concerned with elegant fine prints; after all, craft must not dominate concept. It is clear, however, when viewing Cumming's original prints, that there has been an overall refinement in his craft during the past decade.

One of the most consistently appealing aspects of his photographs is that they are metaphors which can be appreciated on many levels. Robert Cumming is a magician who seems to be explaining the secret to his magic, but is one step ahead of us.

James Alinder

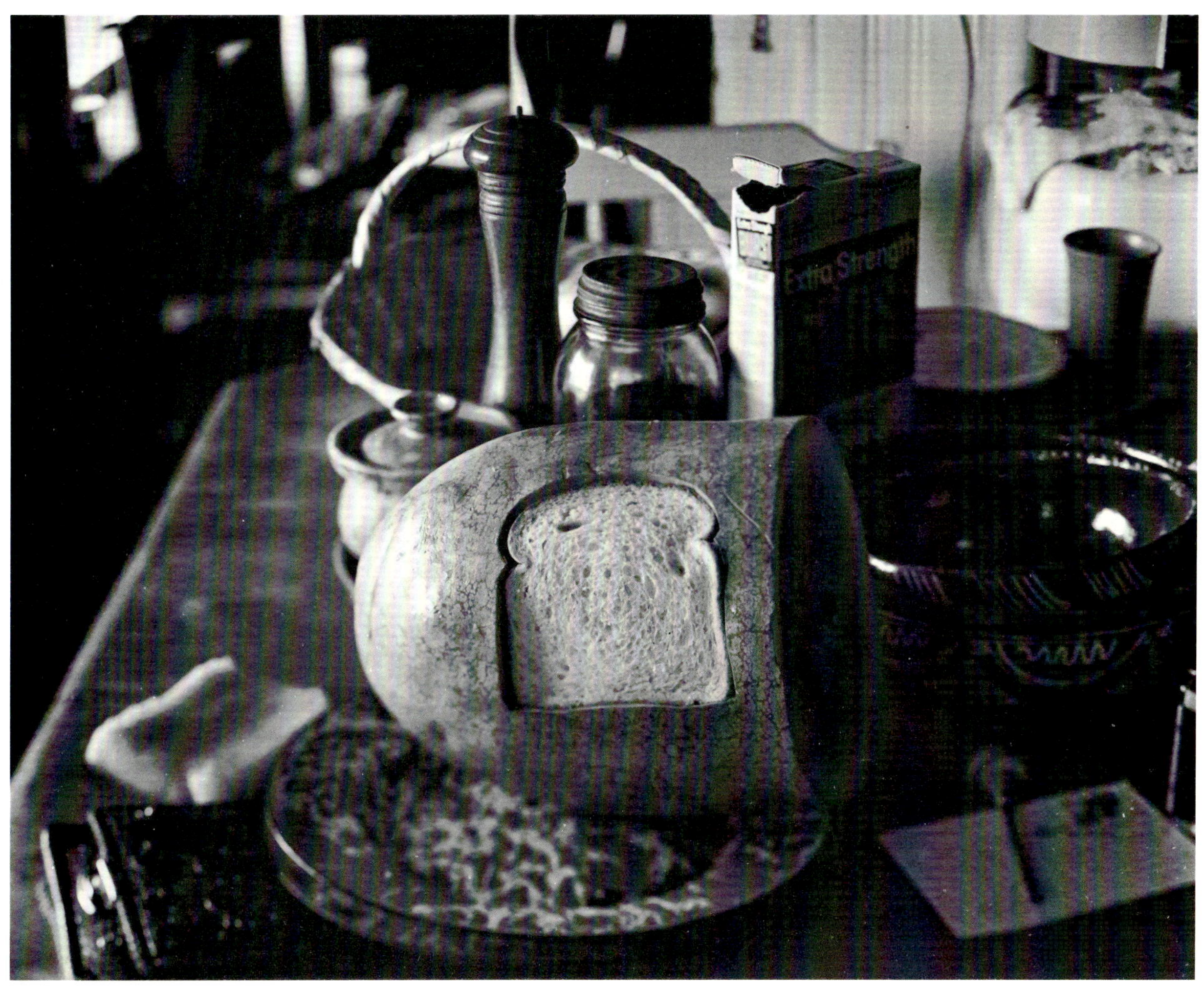

Plate 1: Watermelon/Bread, 1970

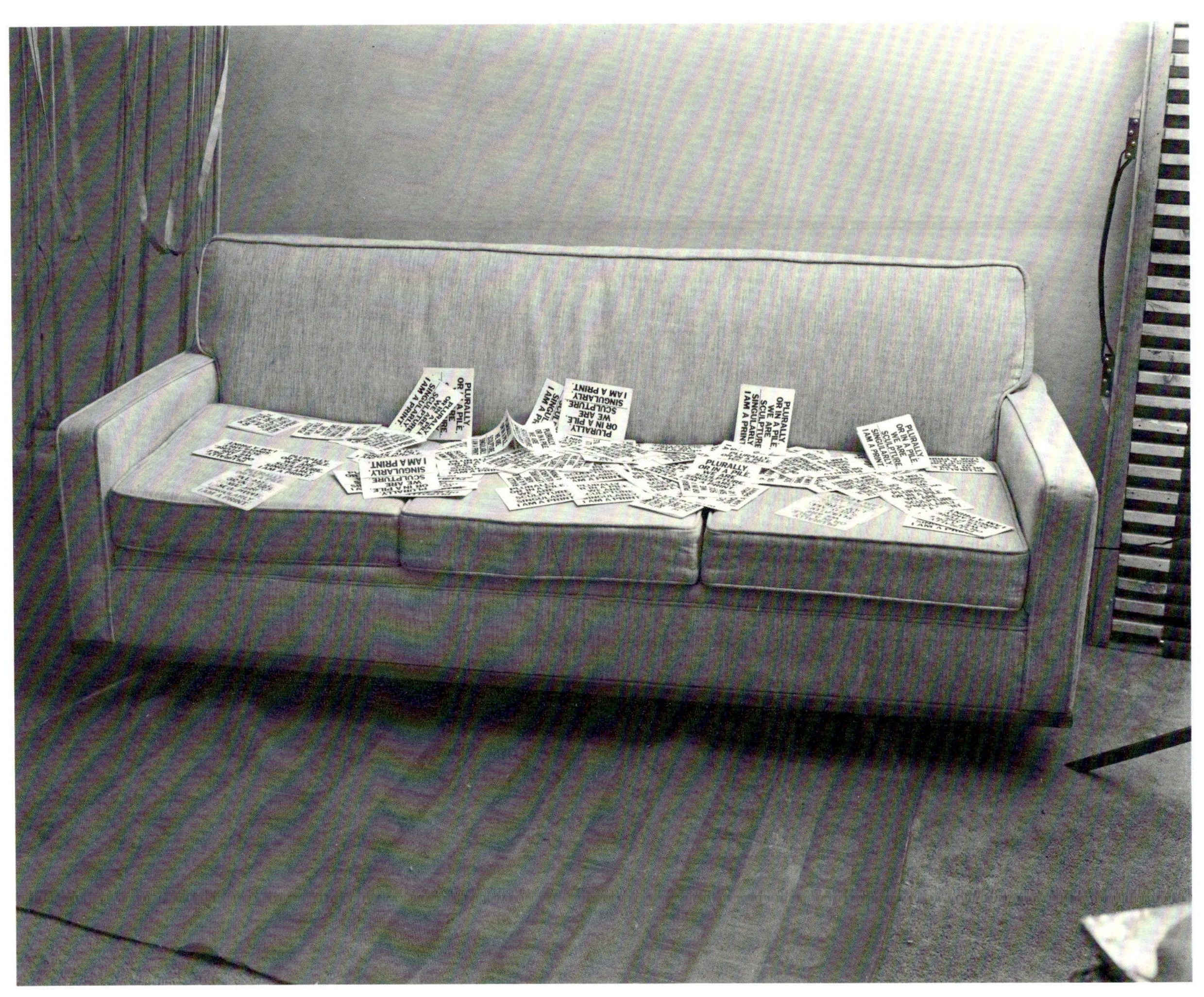

Plate 2: 120 Alternatives, 1970

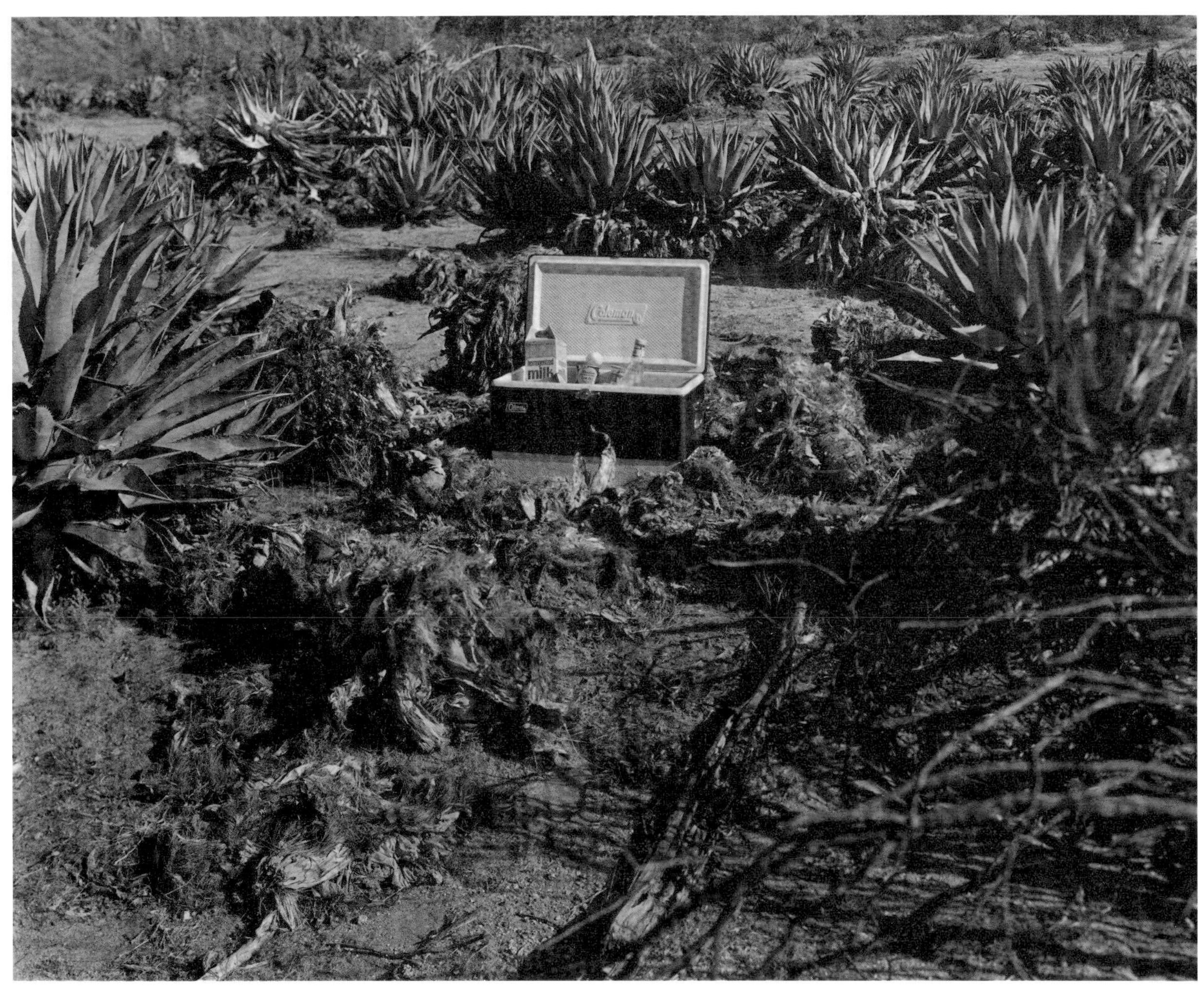

Plate 3: Coleman Cooler, Borrego Desert, California, 1971

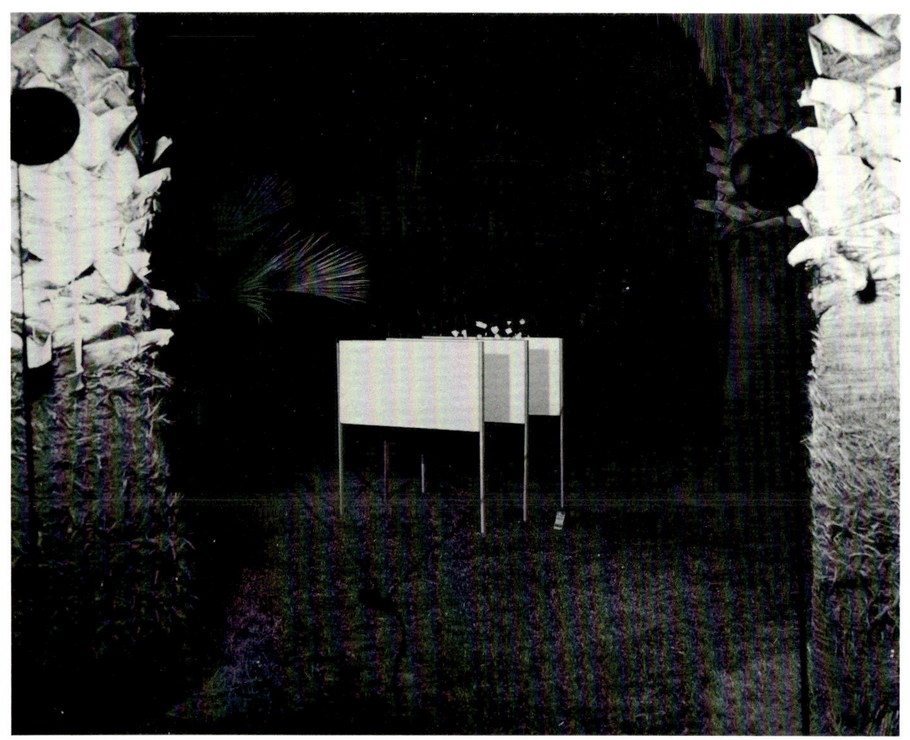

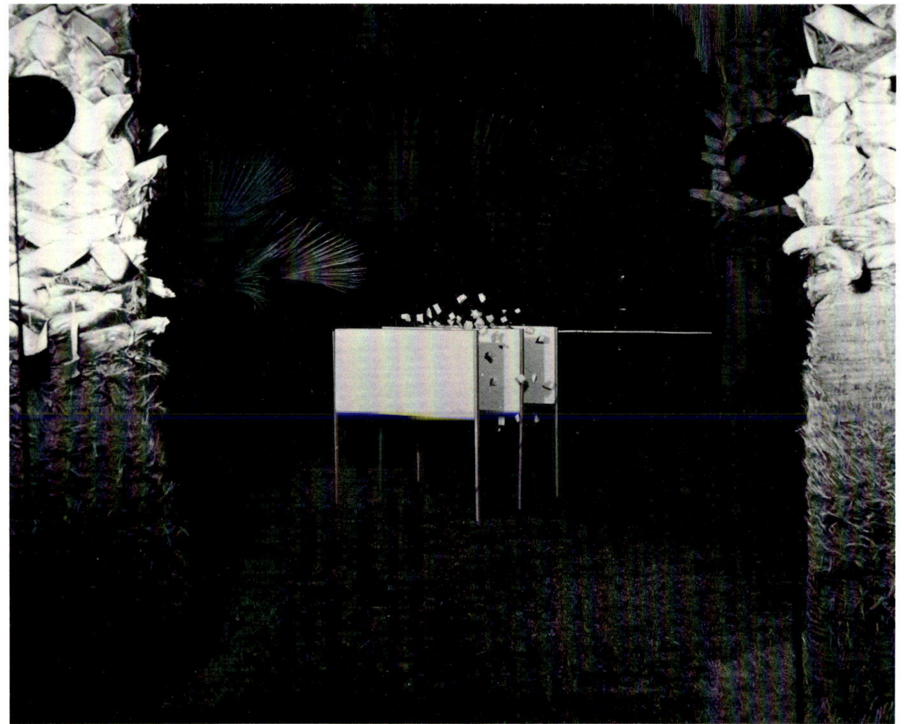

Plates 4, 5, 6 & 7: Blast Sequence, 1973

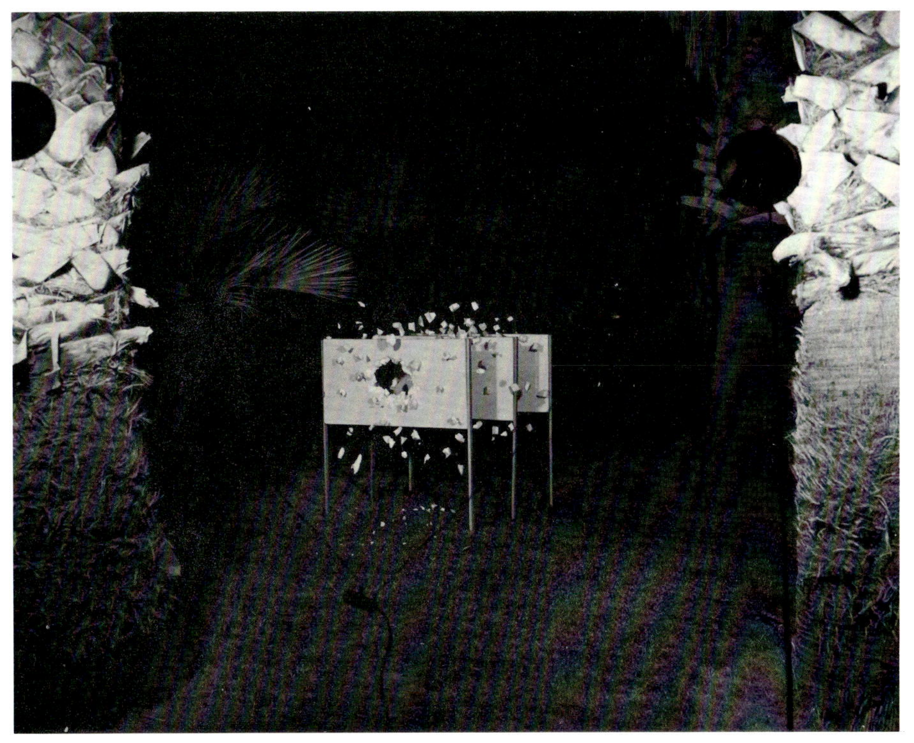

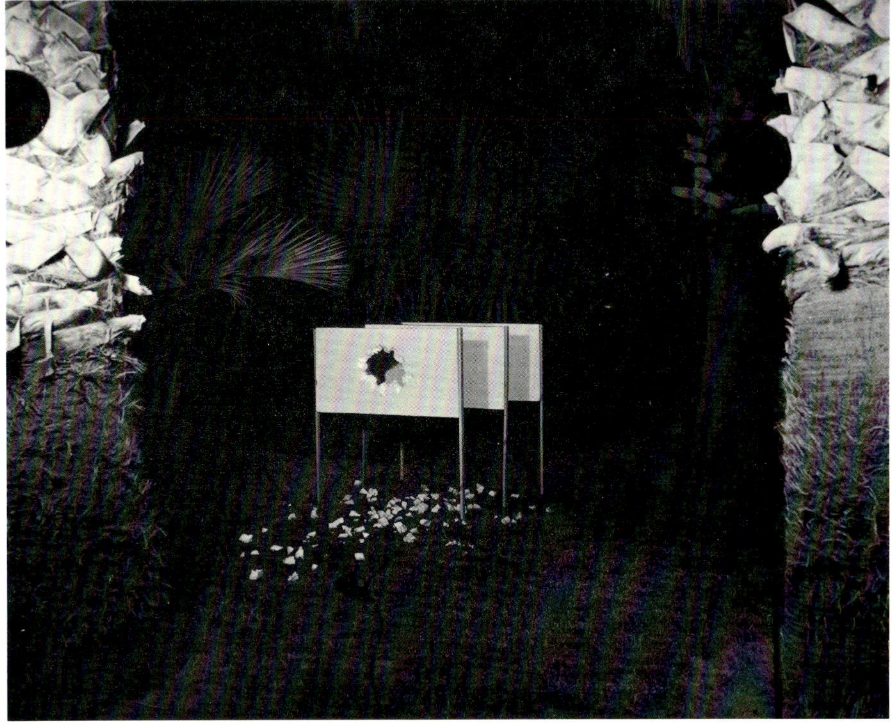

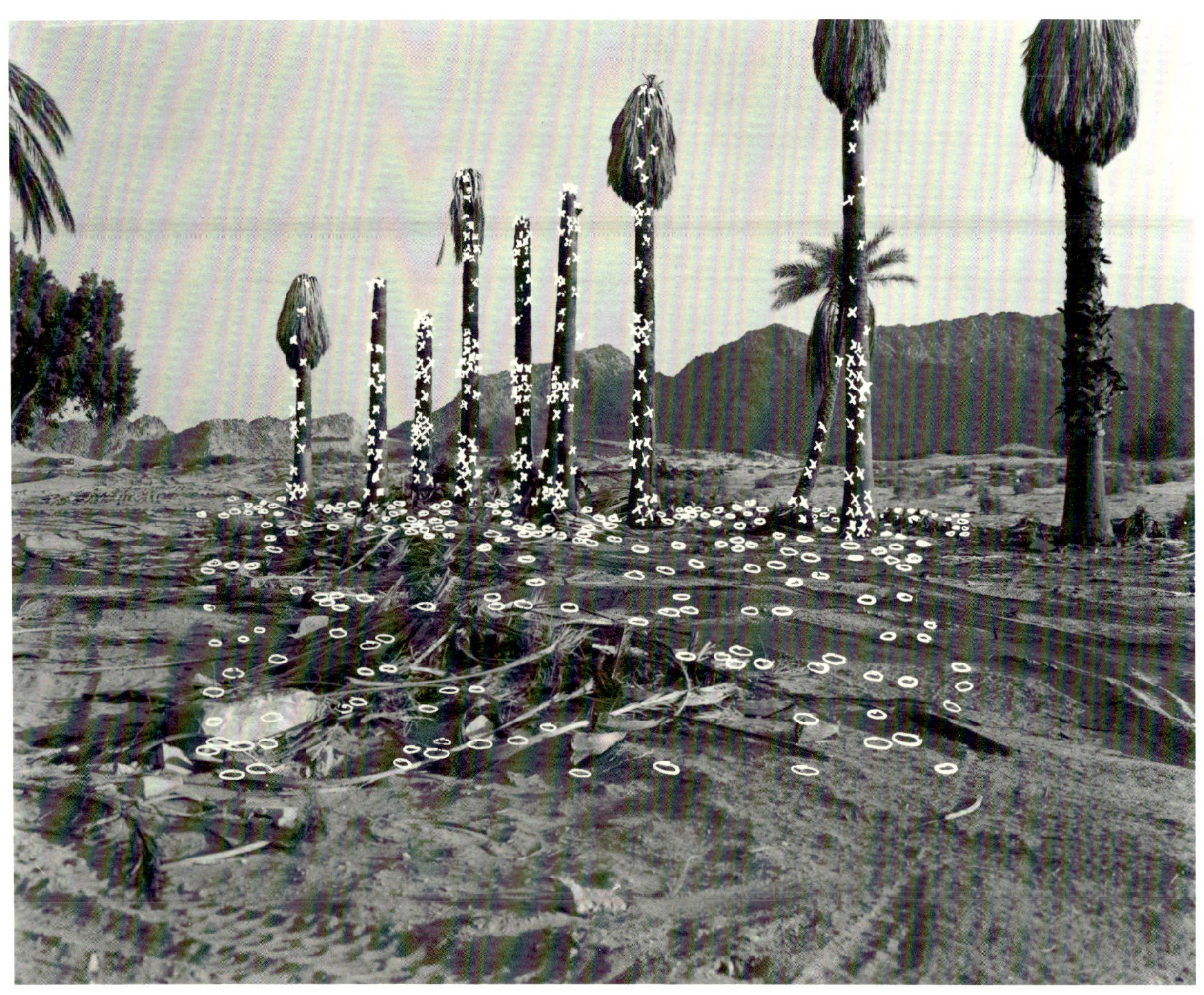

Plates 8 & 9: The Effect at the Center of the Overlay Was Most Pleasing, 1973

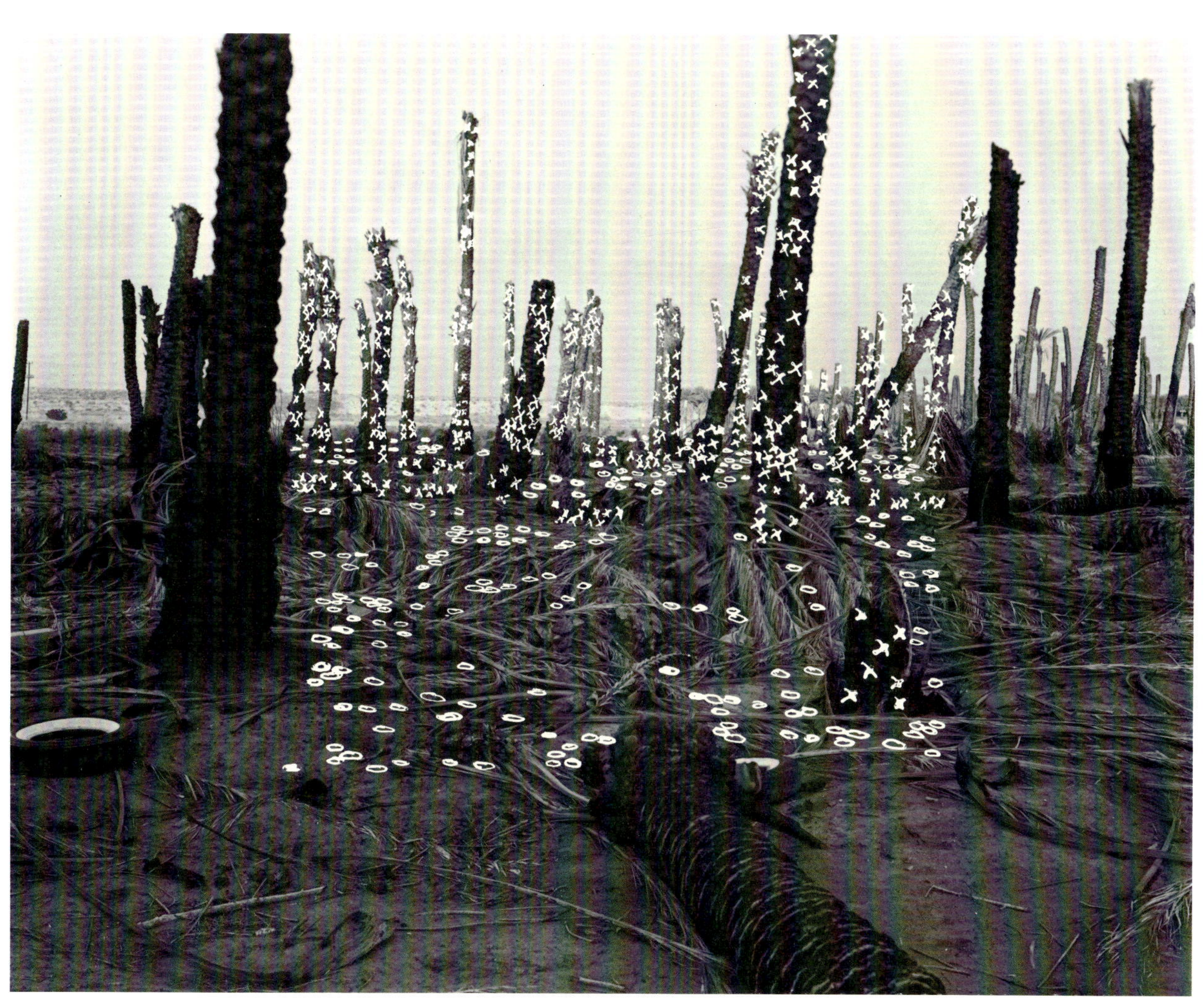

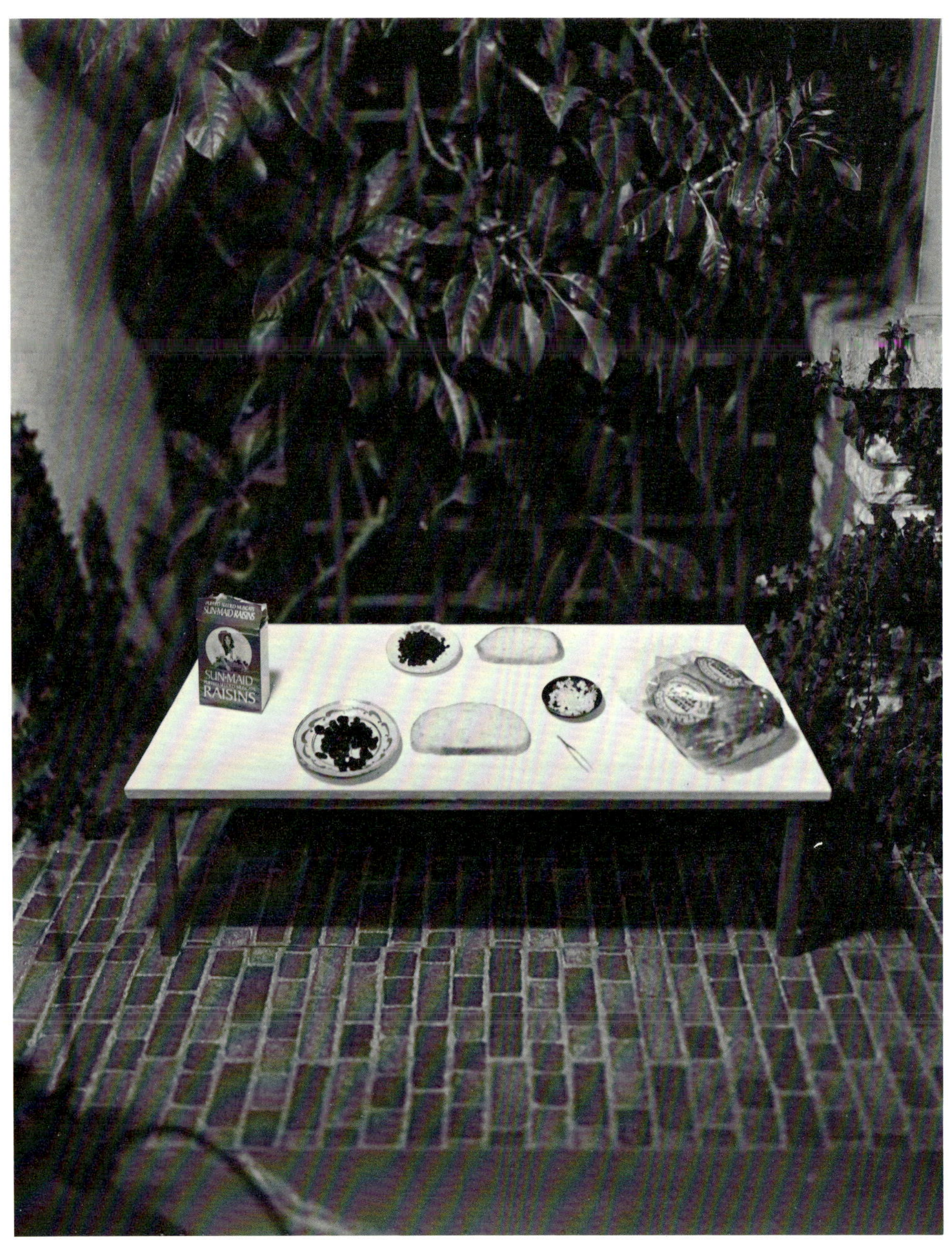

Plates 10 & 11: Ansel Adams Raisin Bread, 1973

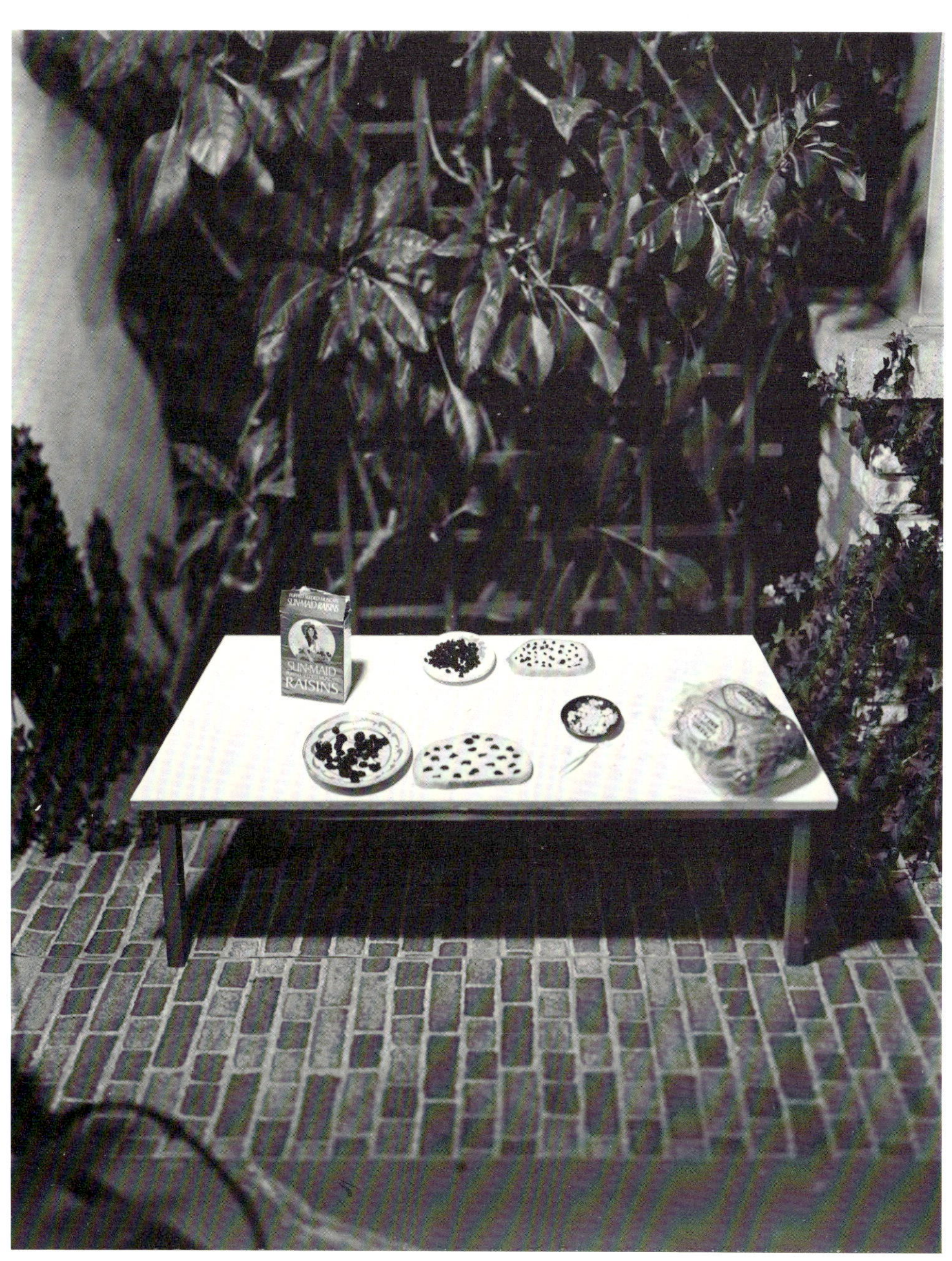
SUN-MAID RAISINS
SUN-MAID
RAISINS

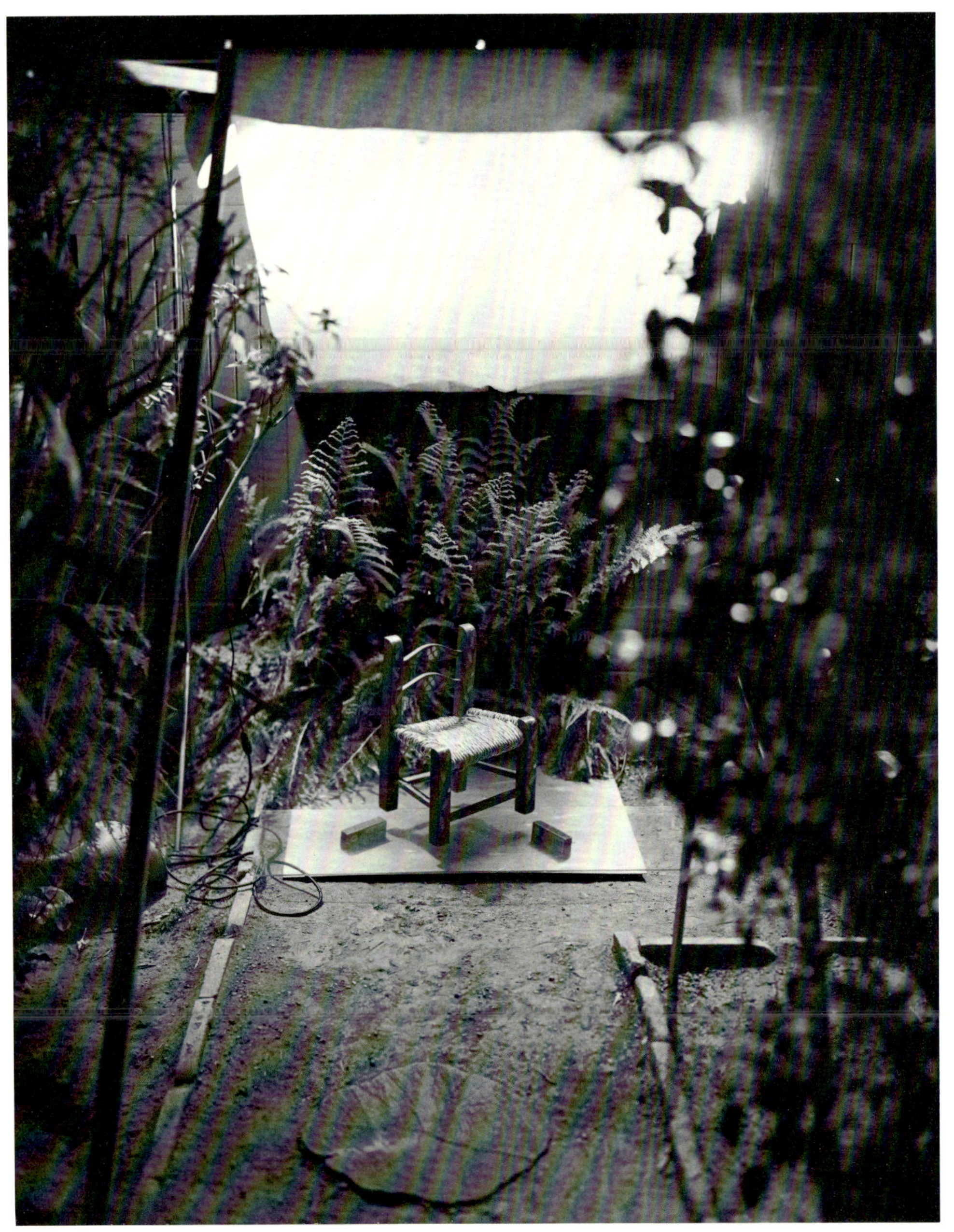

Plate 12: Chair Trick, 1973

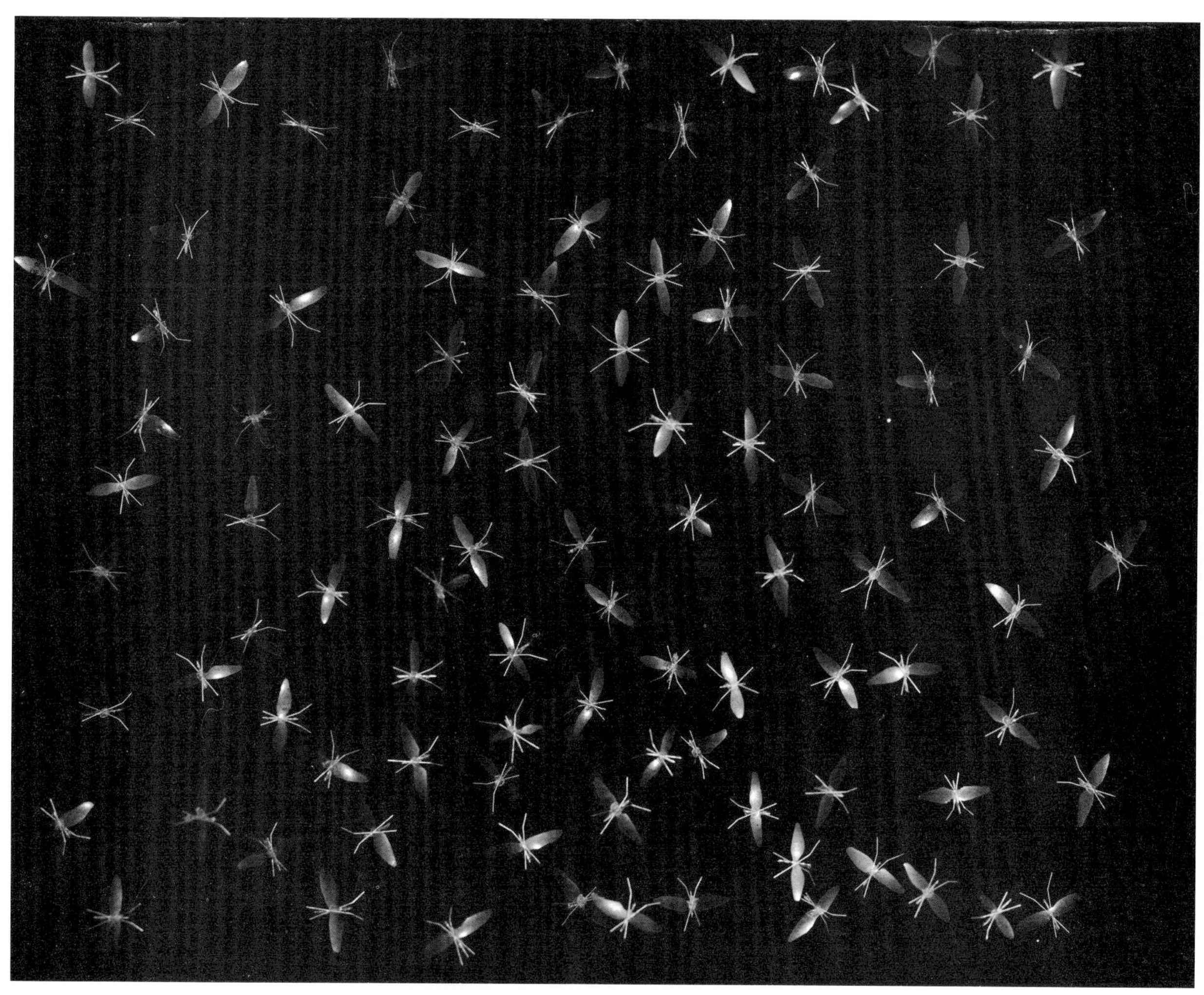

Plate 13: Mosquito Field, 1974

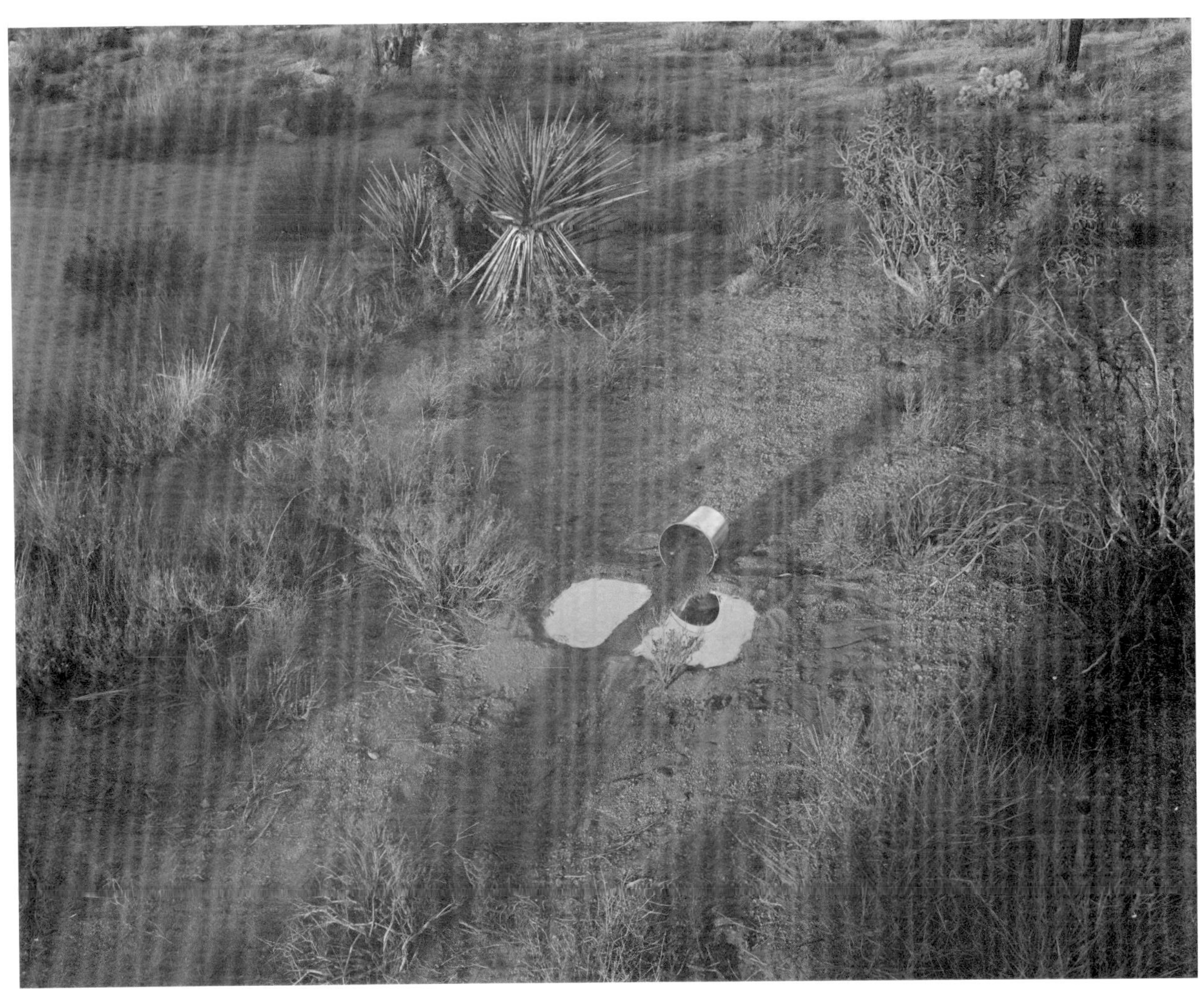

Plates 14 & 15: Two Explanations for a Small, Split Pond, 1974

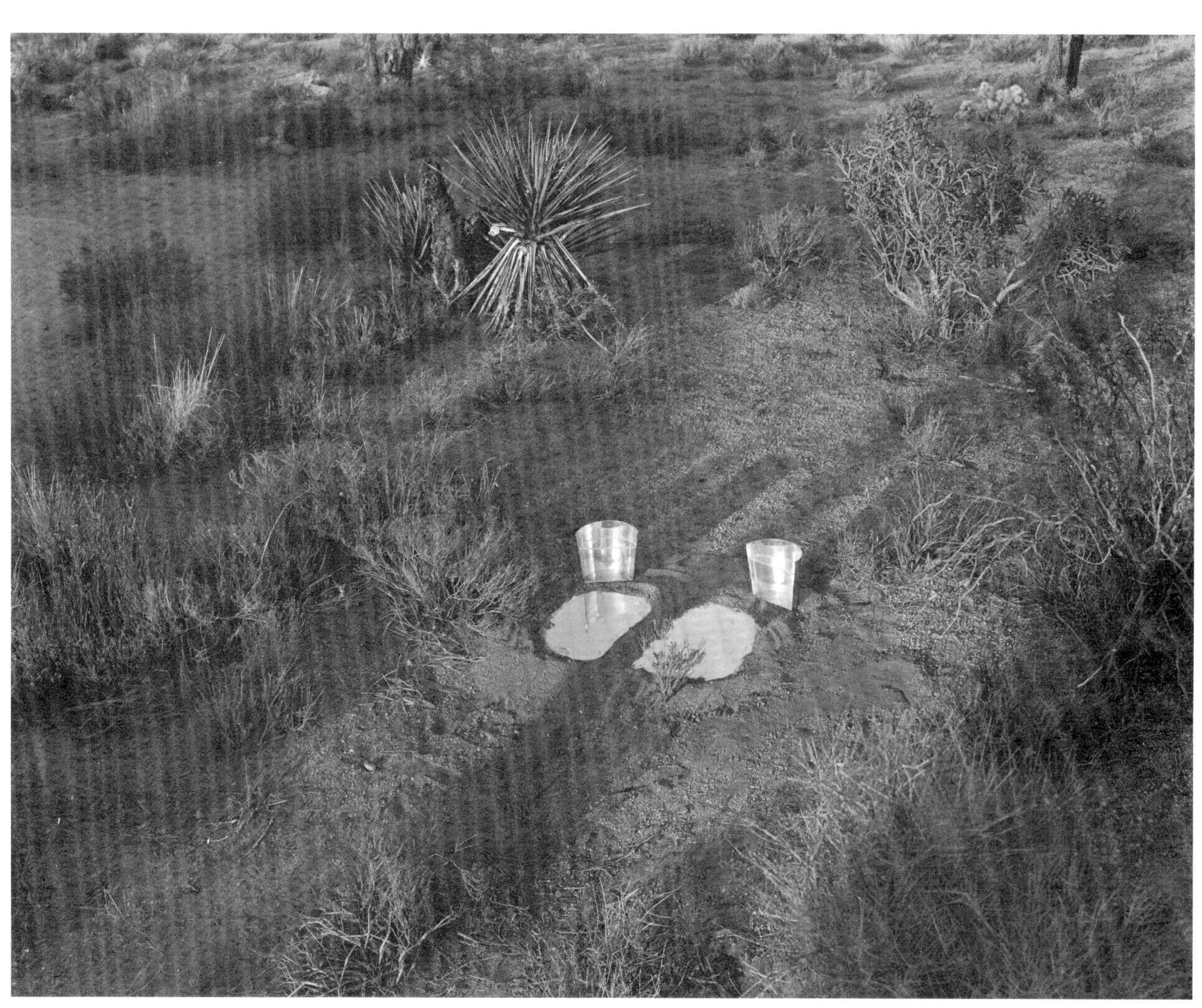

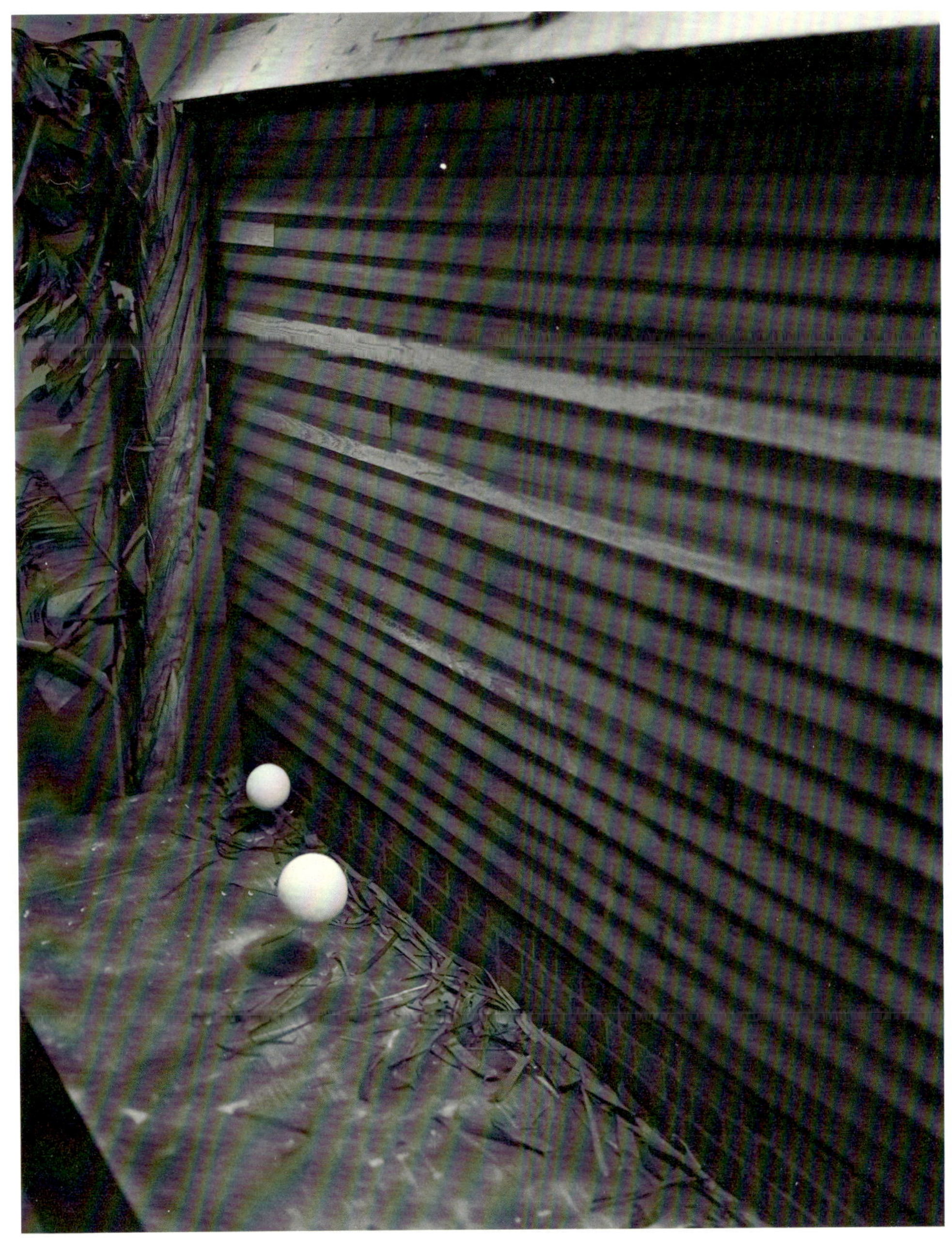

Plates 16 & 17: Of 8 Balls Dropped Off the Peak of the Roof
2 Fell on the North Side, 6 Favored the East, 1974

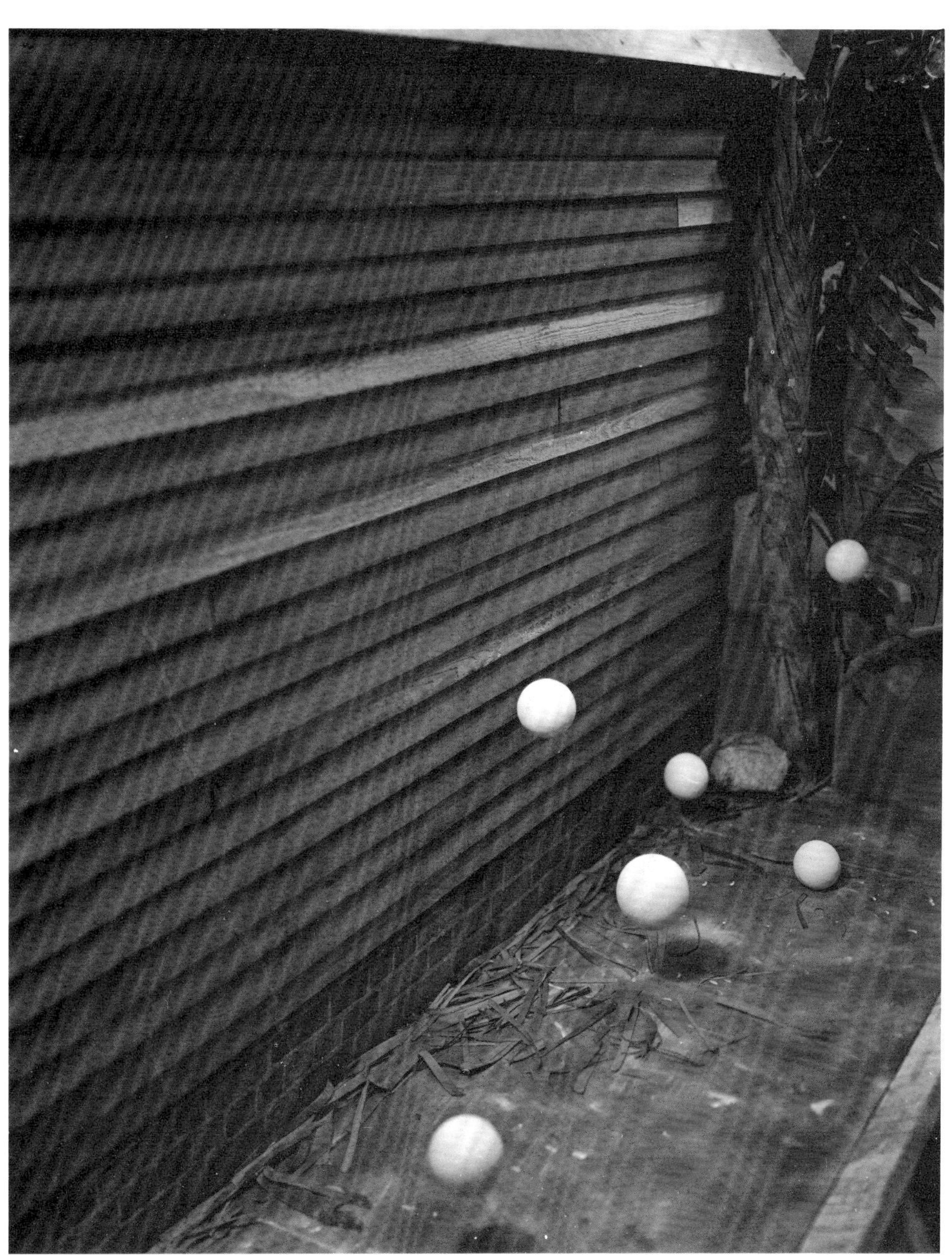

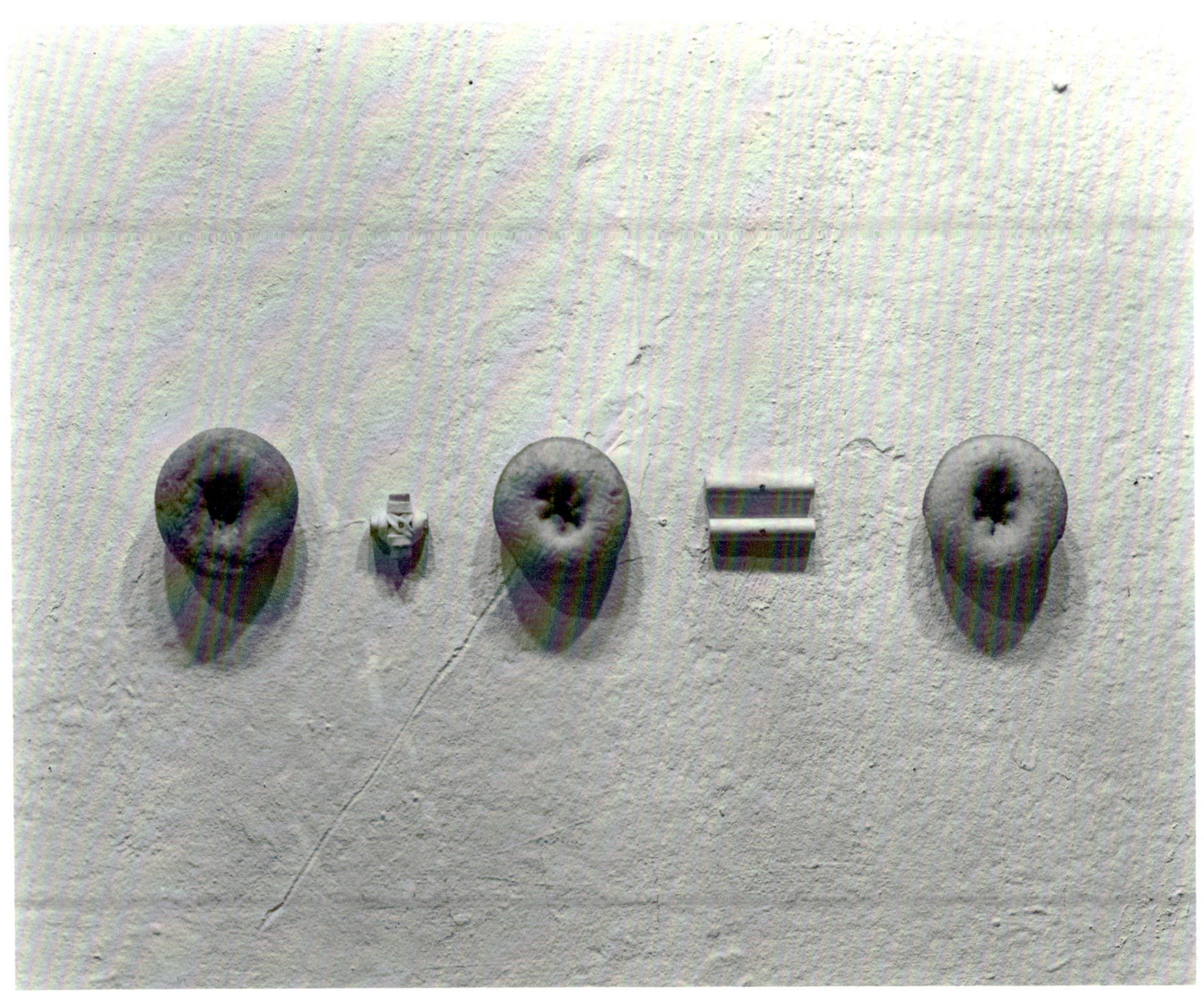

Plates 18 & 19: Zero Plus Zero Equals Zero
A Doughnut Plus a Doughnut Equals Two Doughnuts, 1974

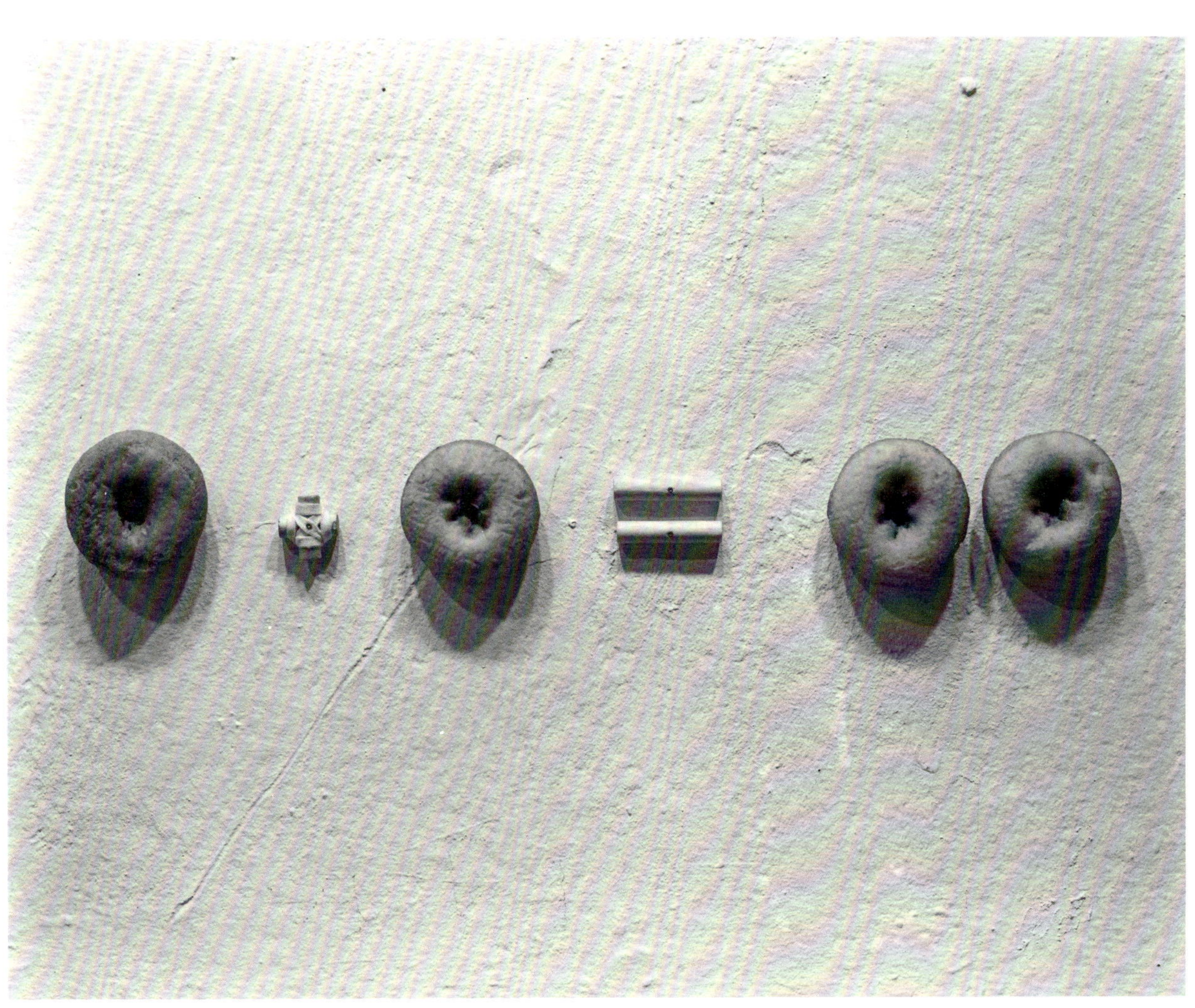

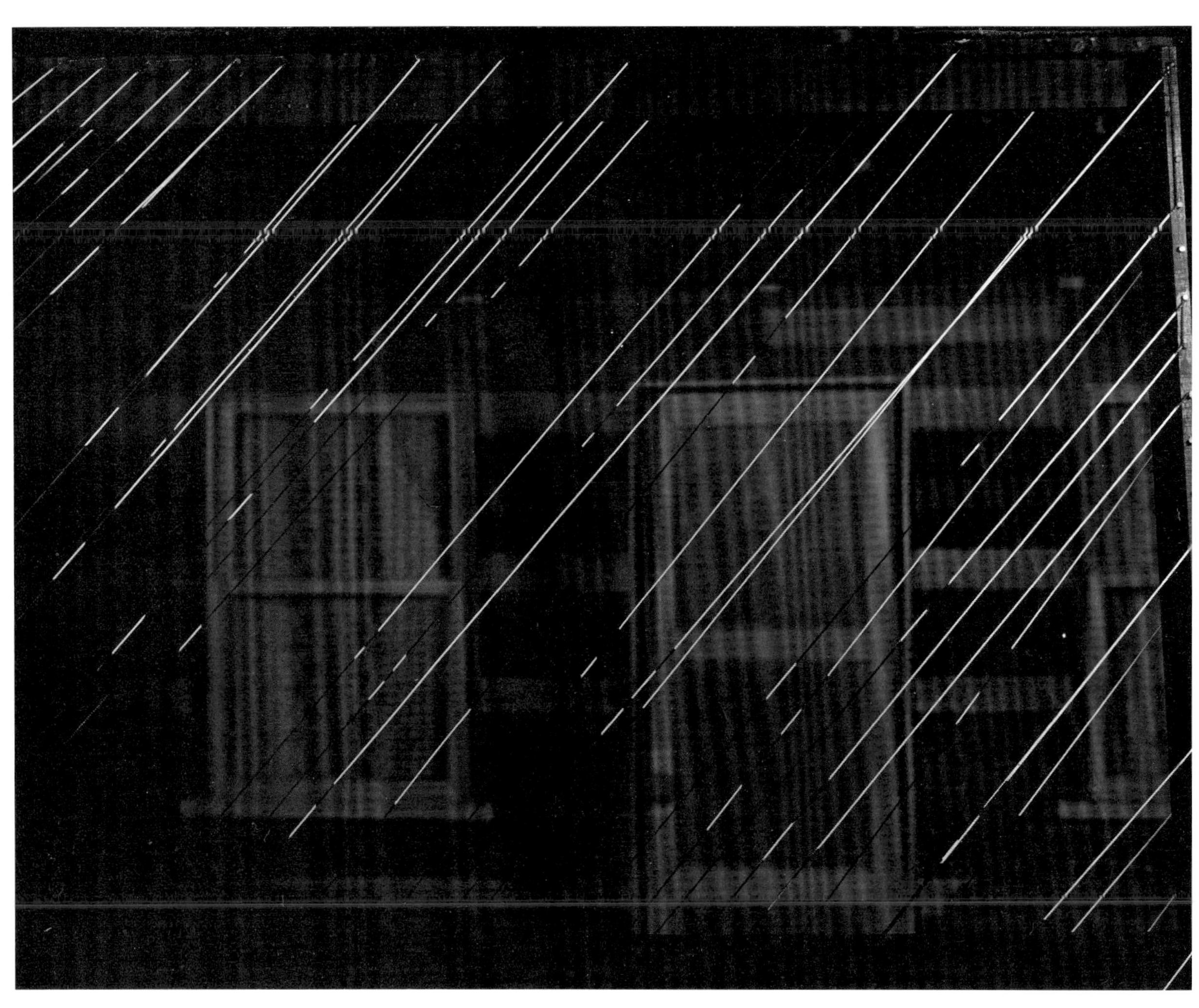

Plates 20 & 21: Fast and Slow Rain—Driving Rain and Downpour, 1974

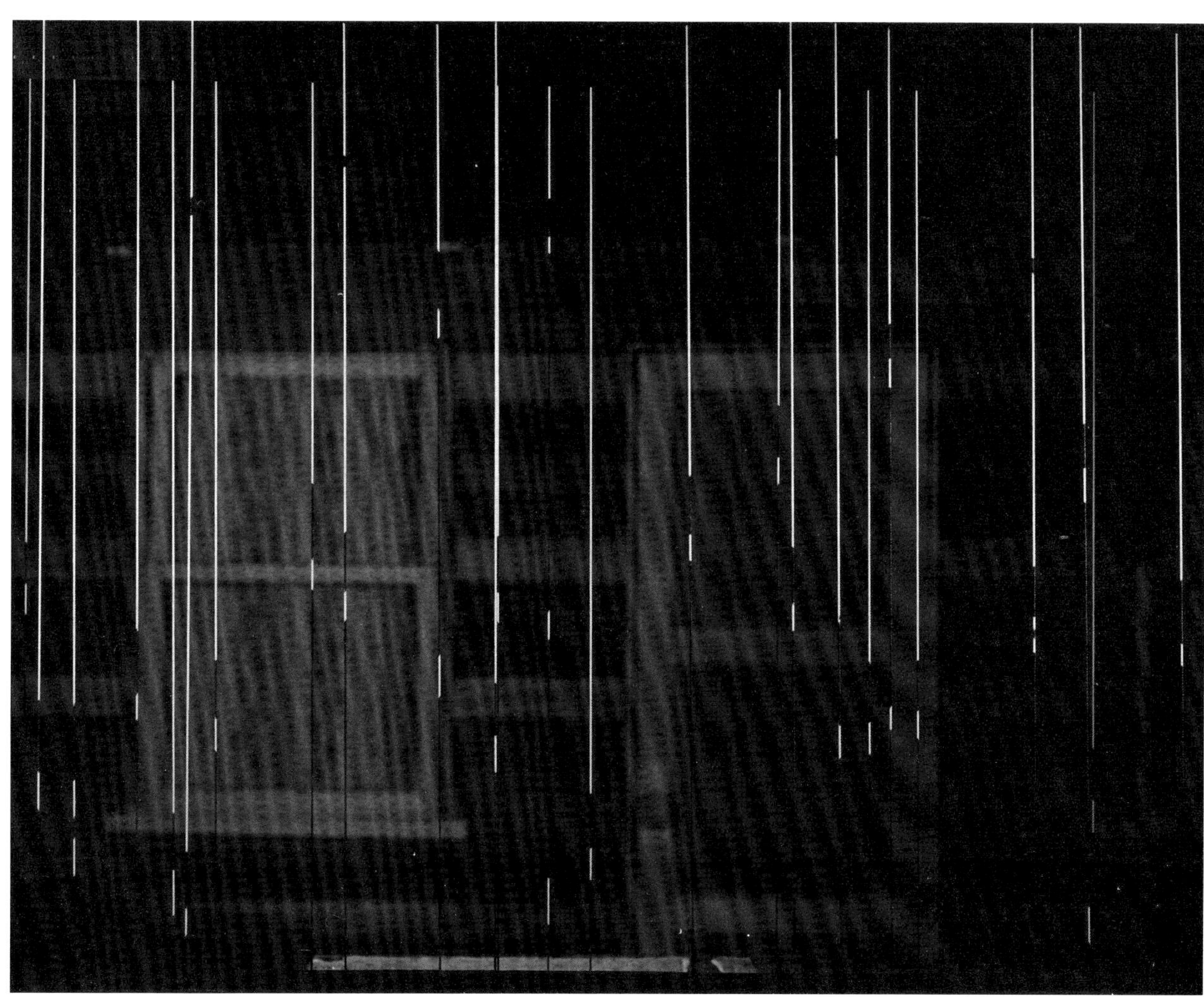

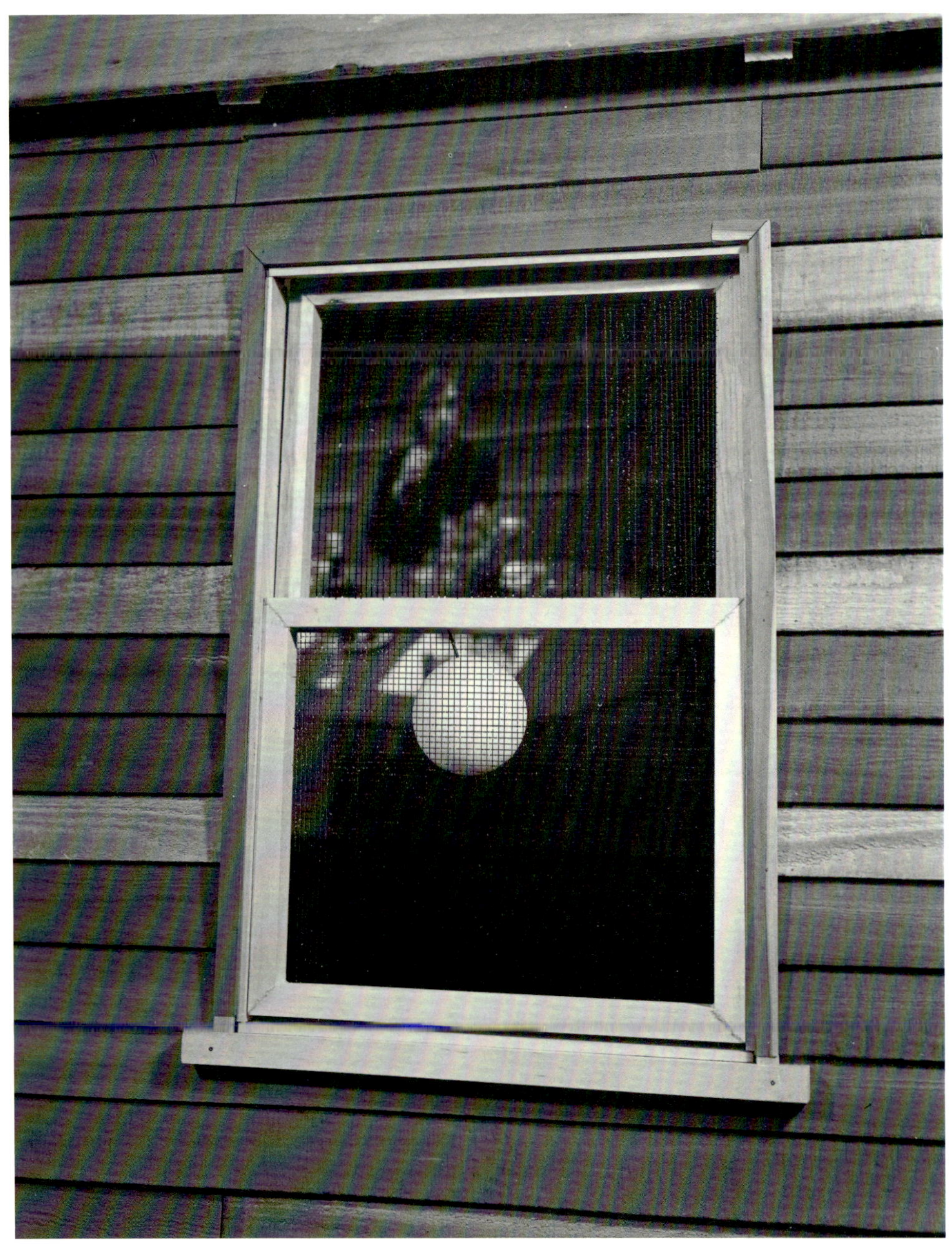

Plates 22 & 23: It Was Around Dinner When the Ball Went through the Screen, 1974

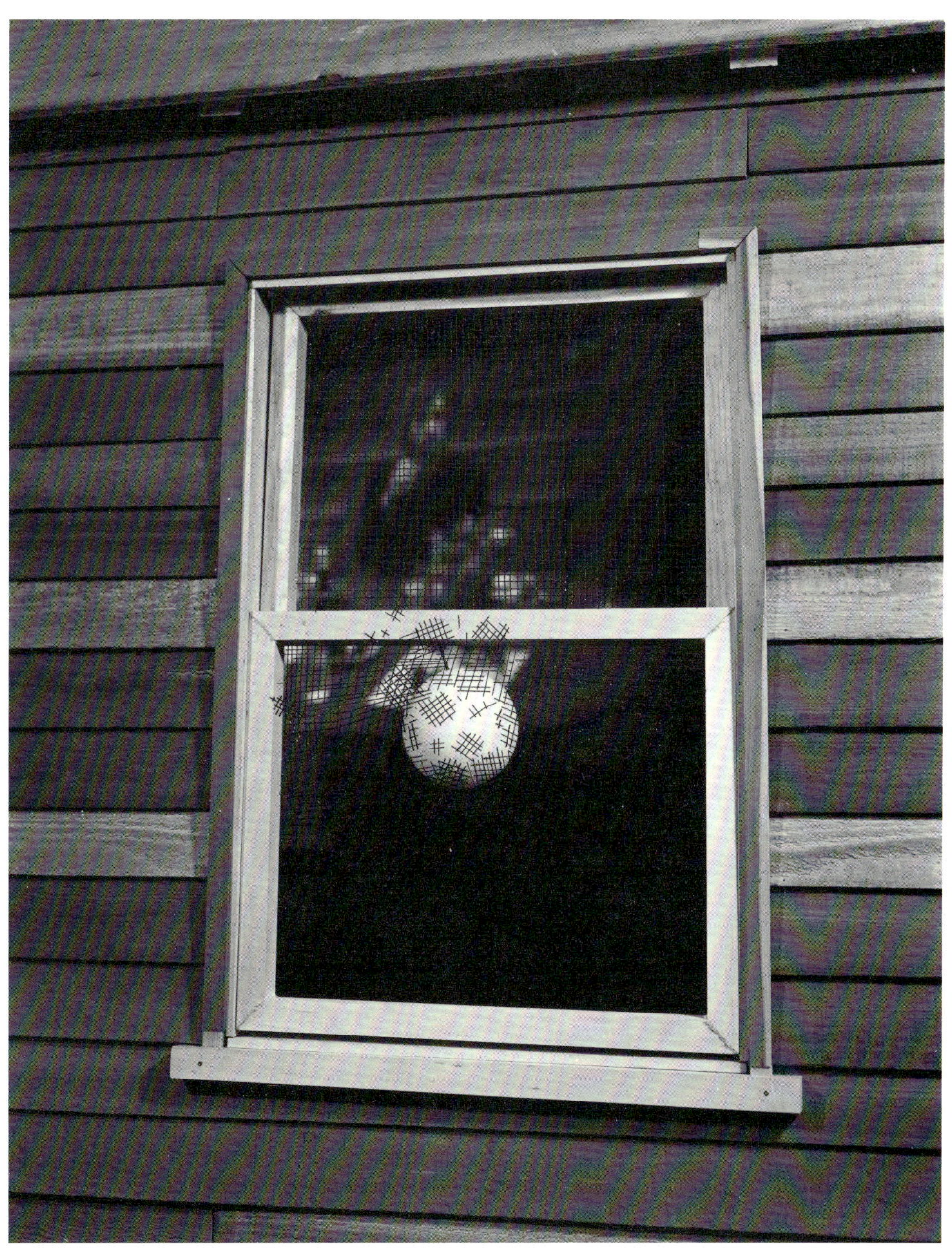

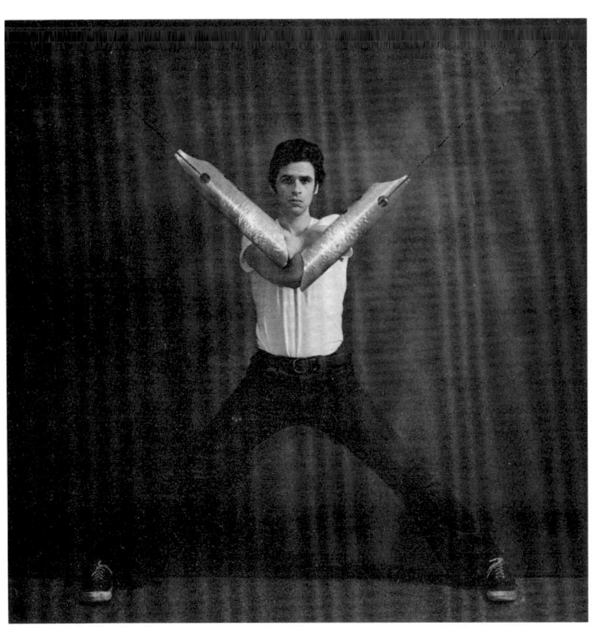

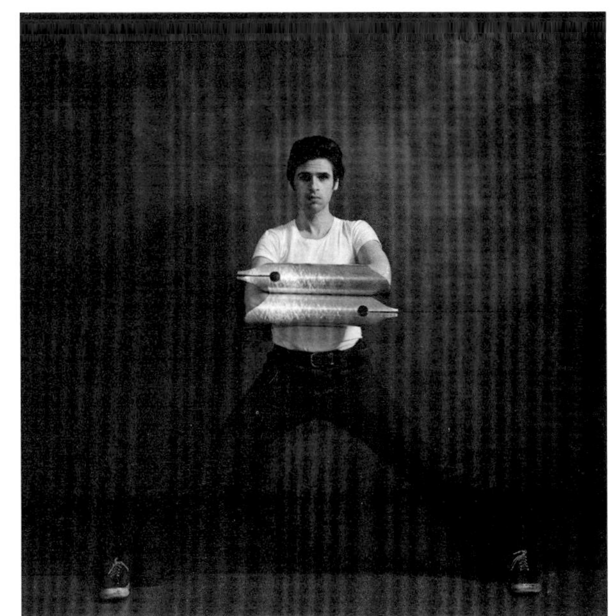

Plates 24, 25, 26 & 27: Cross-body, Pen-point Choreography, 1975

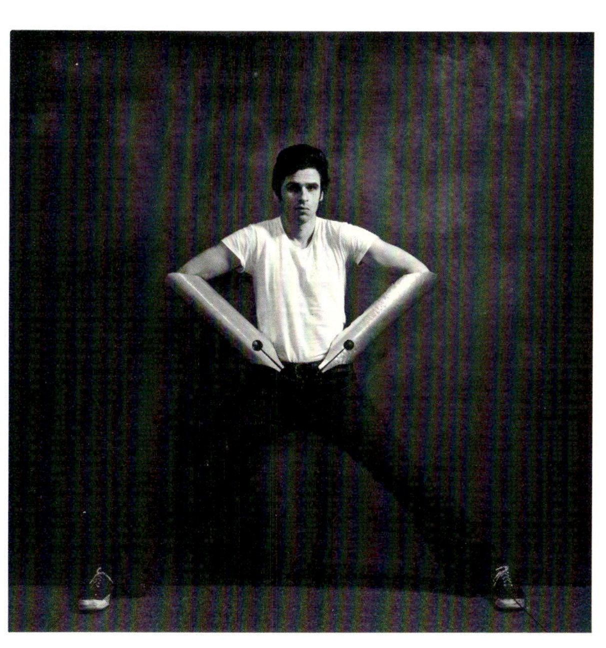

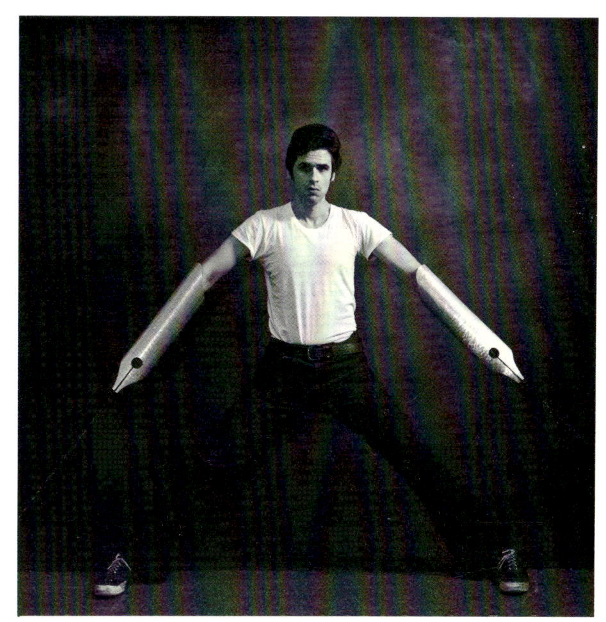

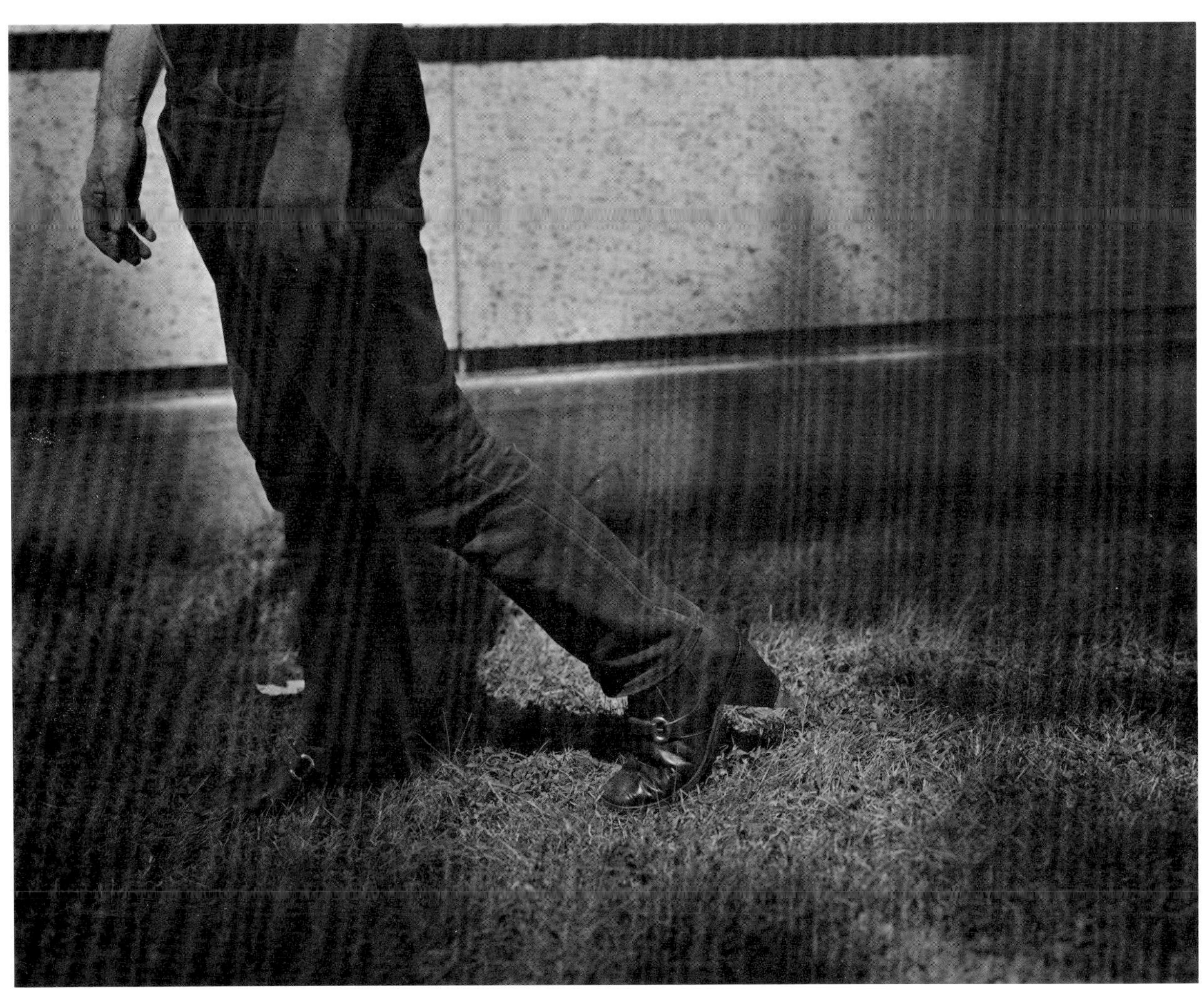

Plates 28 & 29: Distracted in Mid-stride; Spike-heeled Man Kneels to Read, 1975

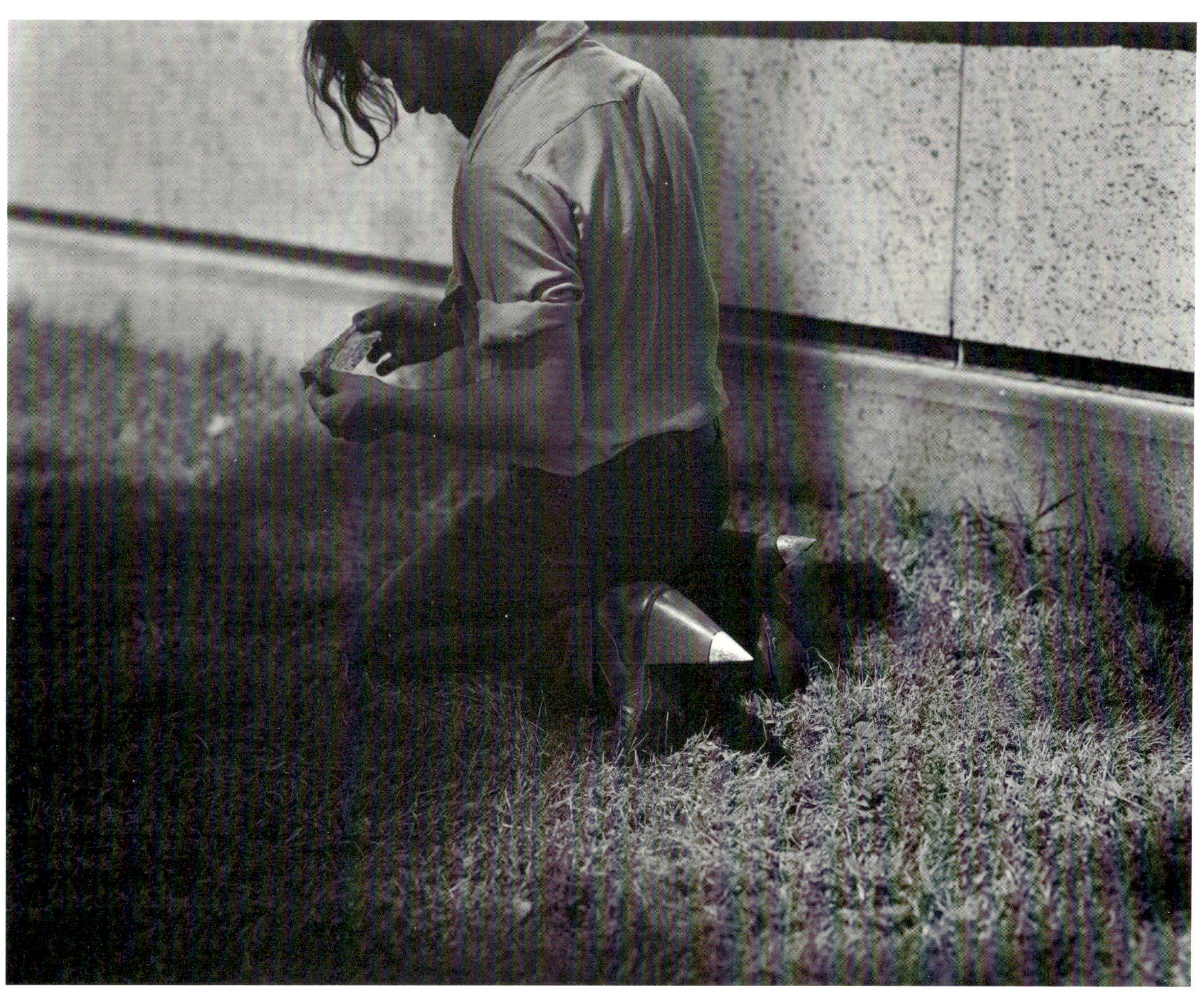

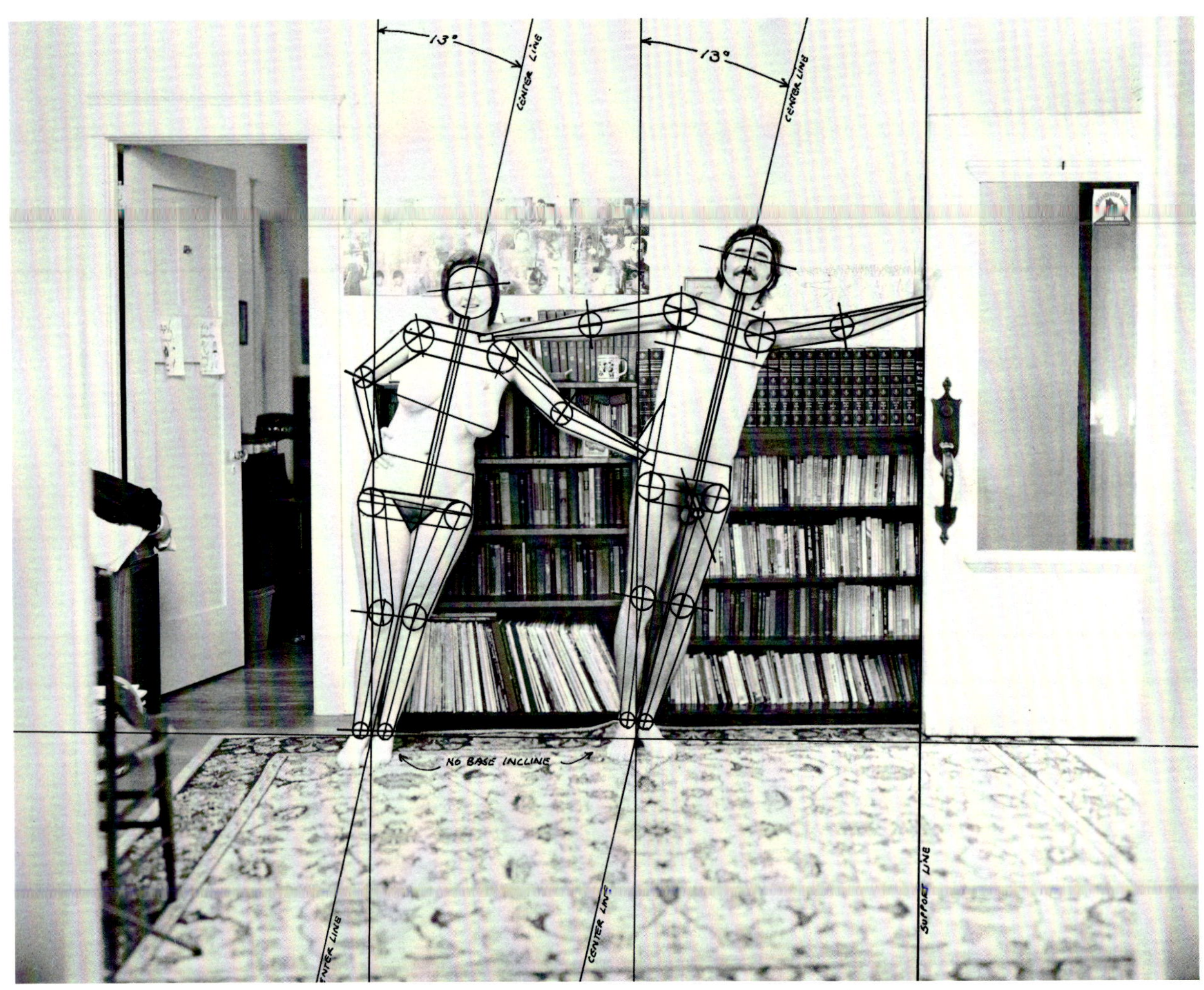

Plates 30 & 31: Leaning Structures, 1975

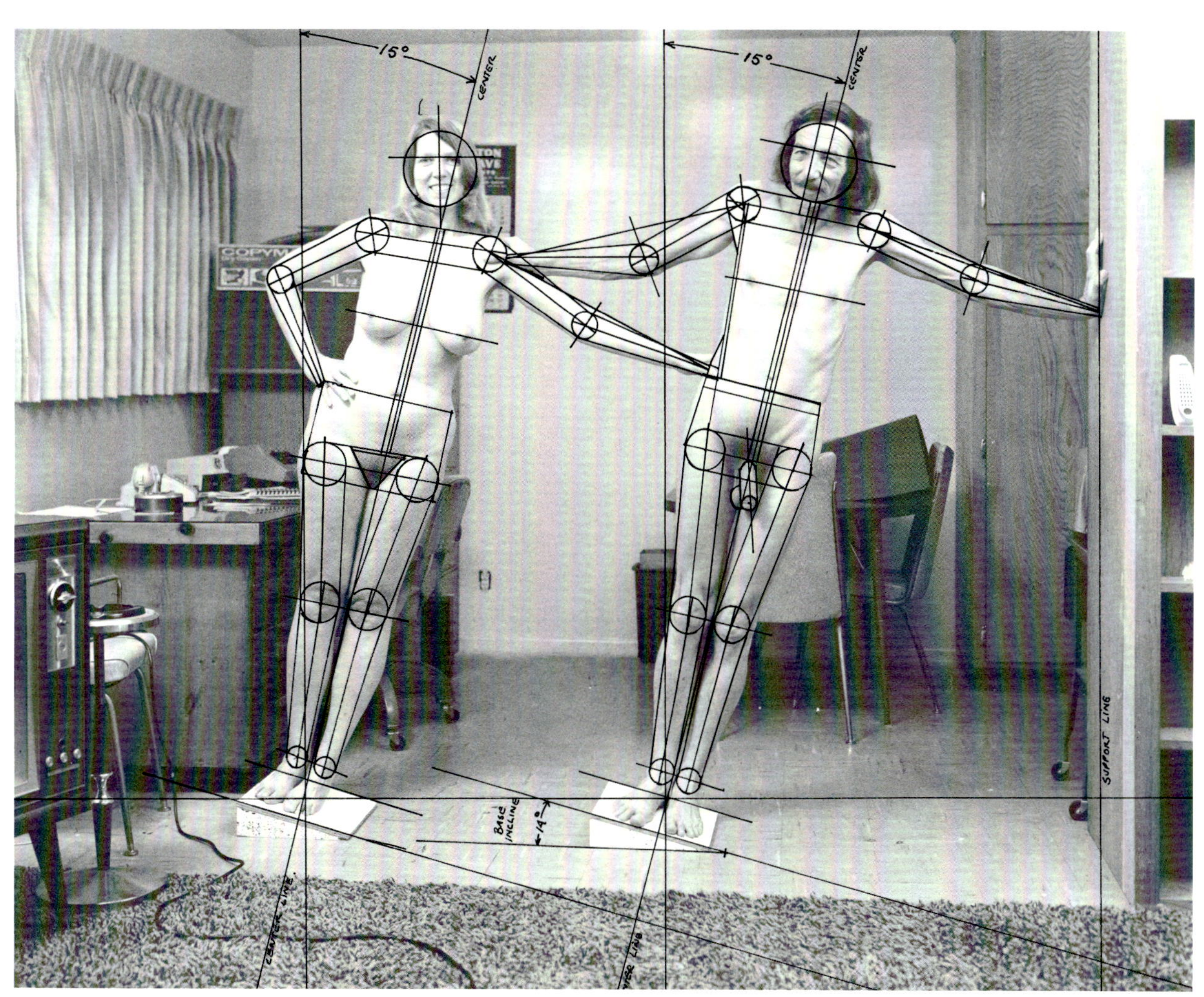

15°
CENTER
15°
CENTER
BASE INCLINE
14°
SUPPORT LINE
CENTER LINE

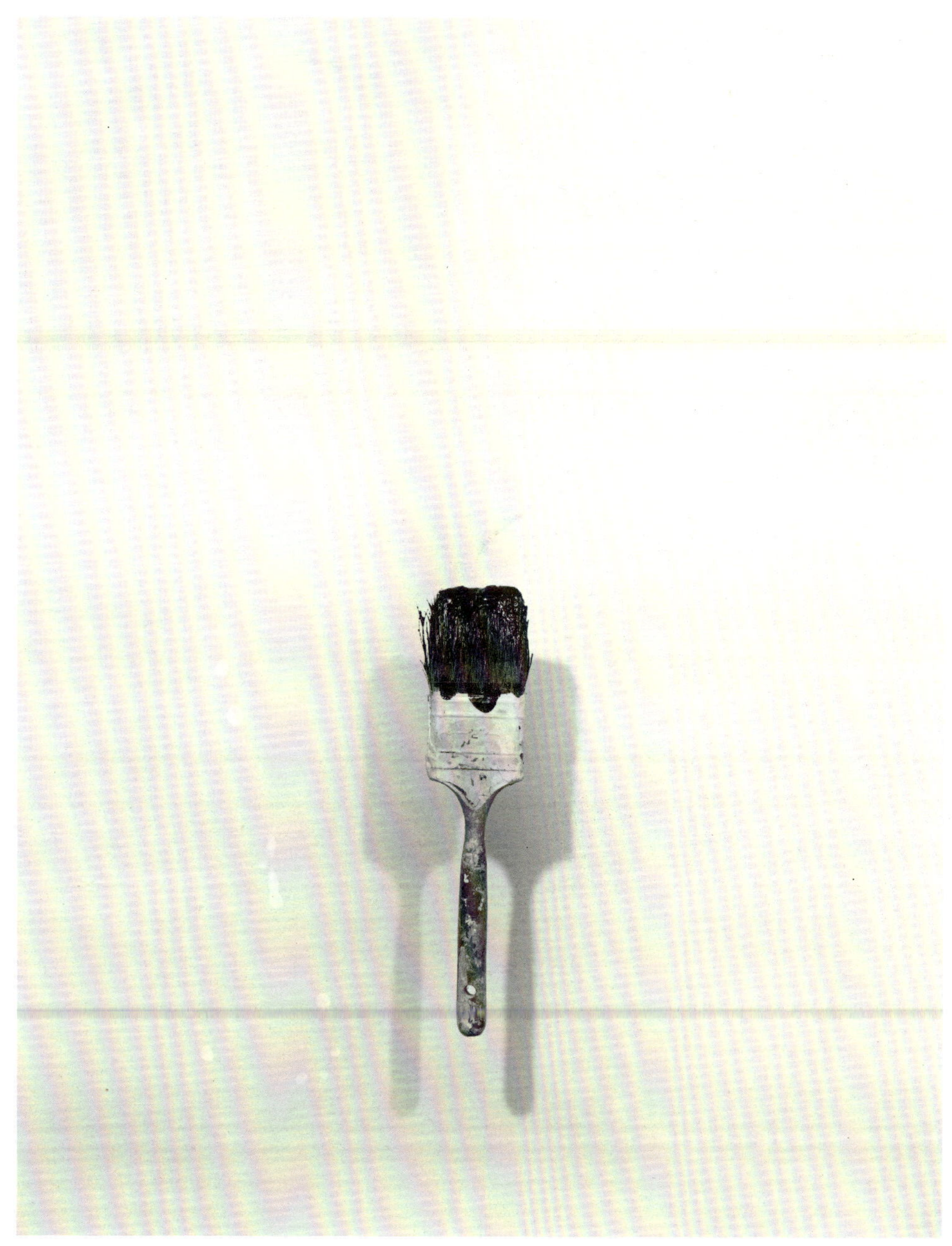

Plates 32 & 33: Exploding Paintbrush, 1975

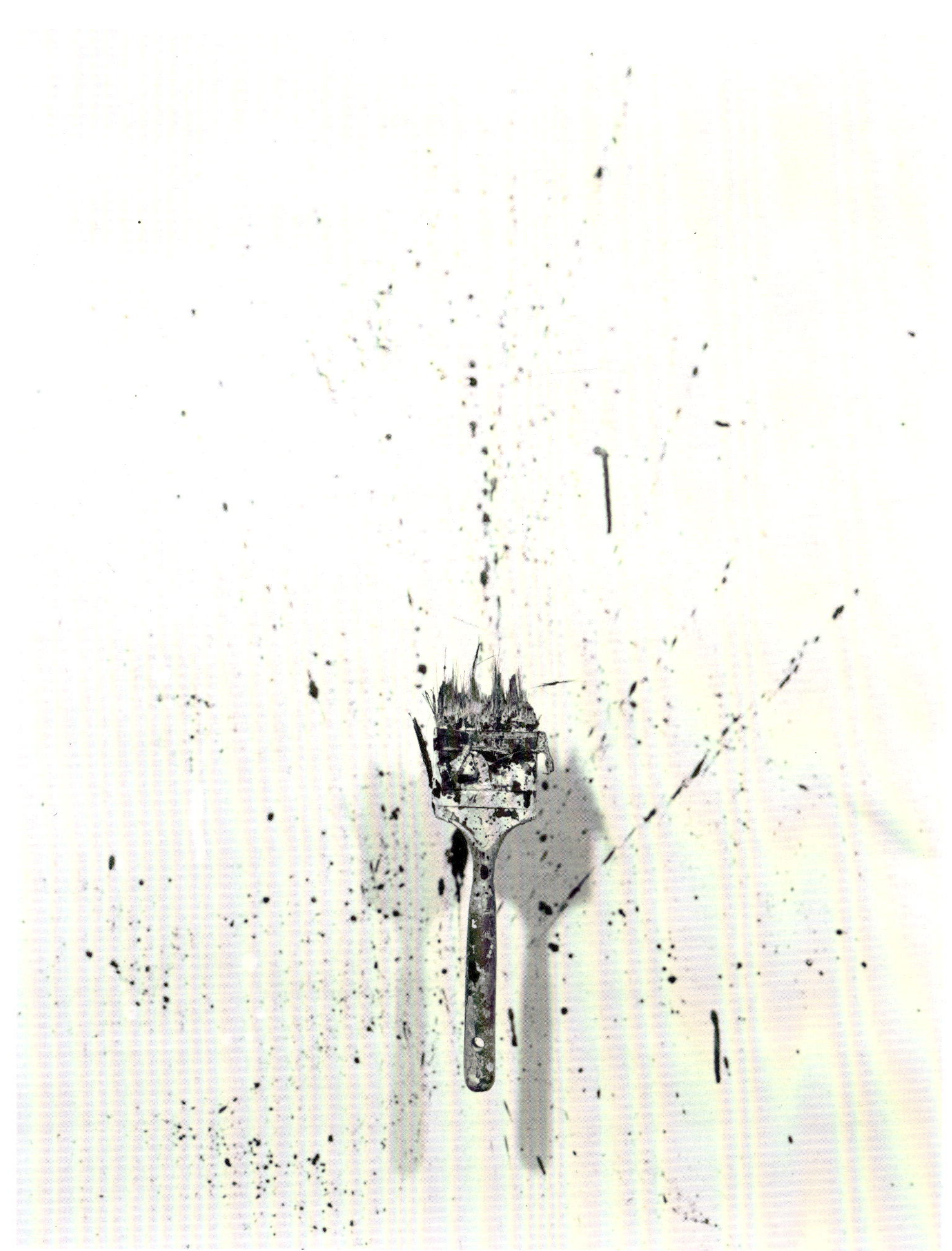

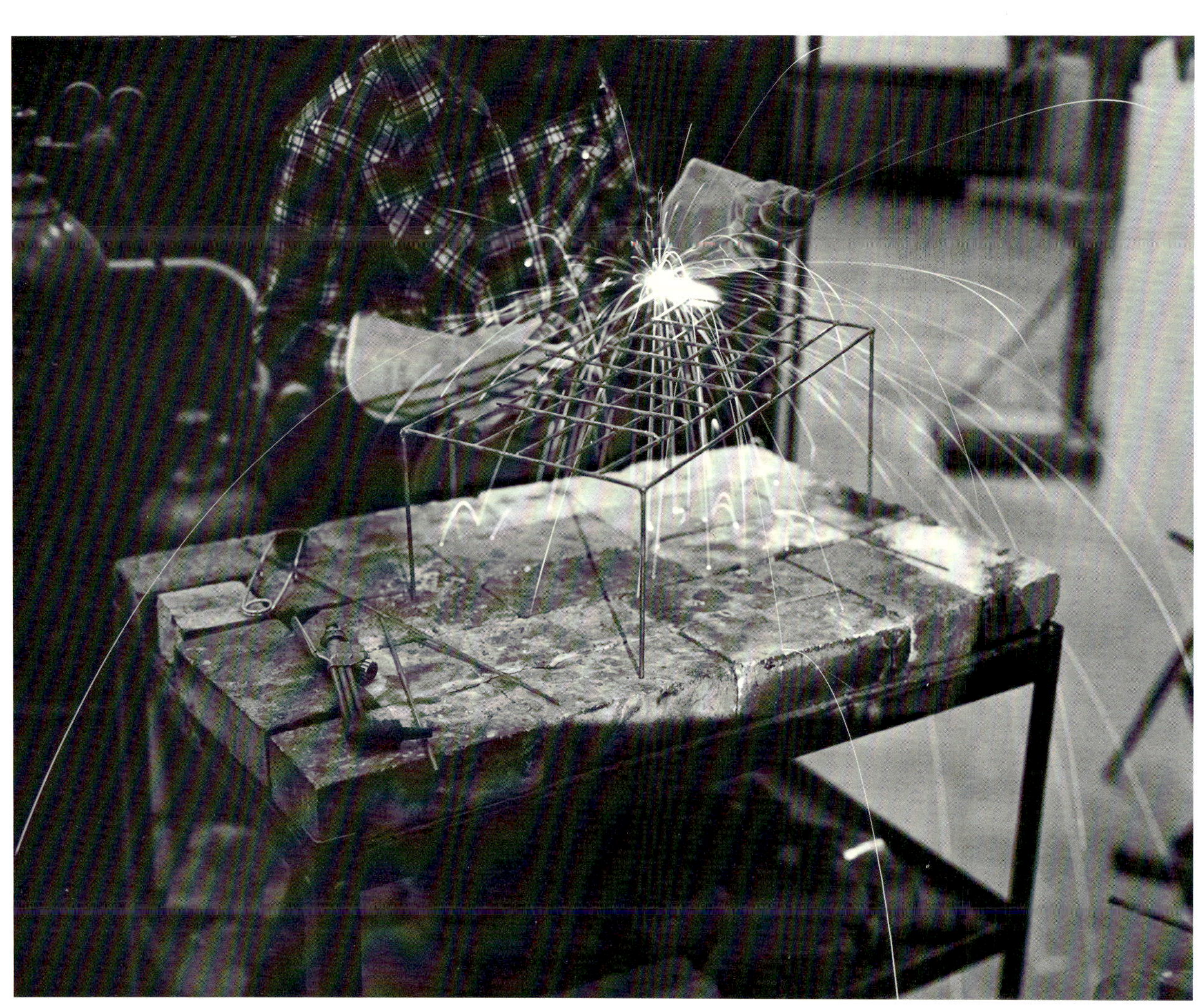

Plates 34 & 35: Energy Transforms Matter, 1977

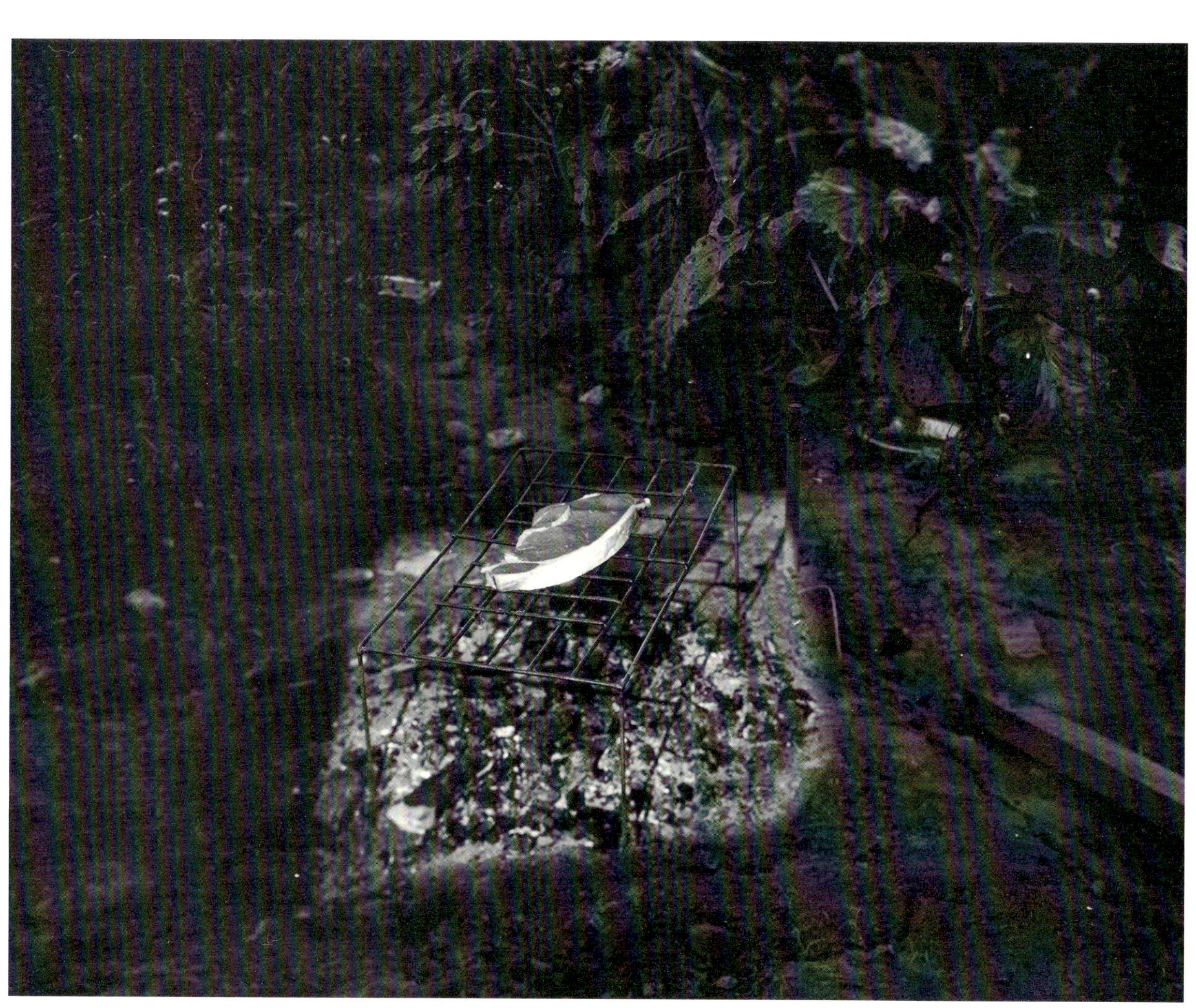

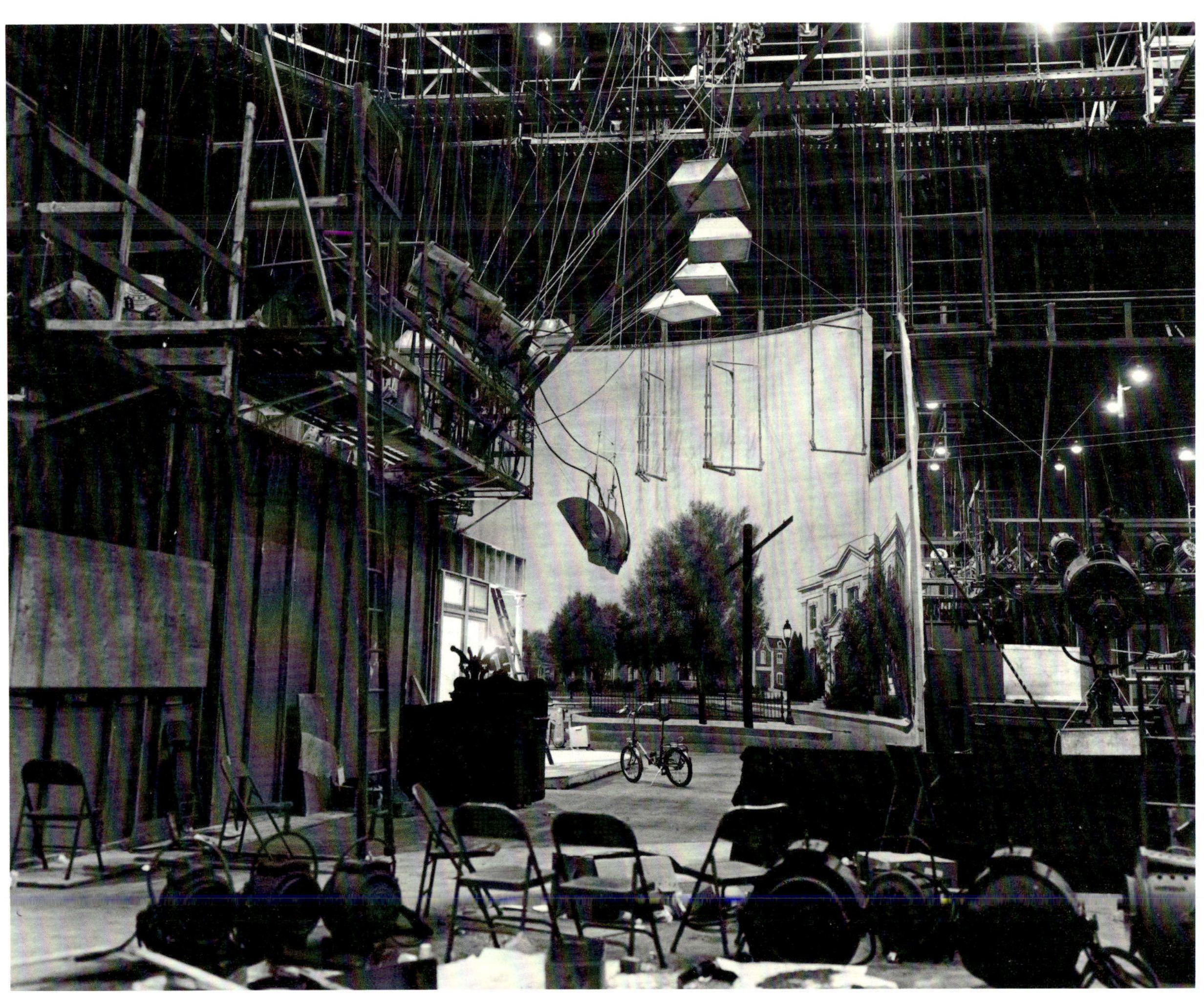

Plate 36: Drugstore and Street; Feature Film, "The Great Gift", Stage #12, June 1, 1977

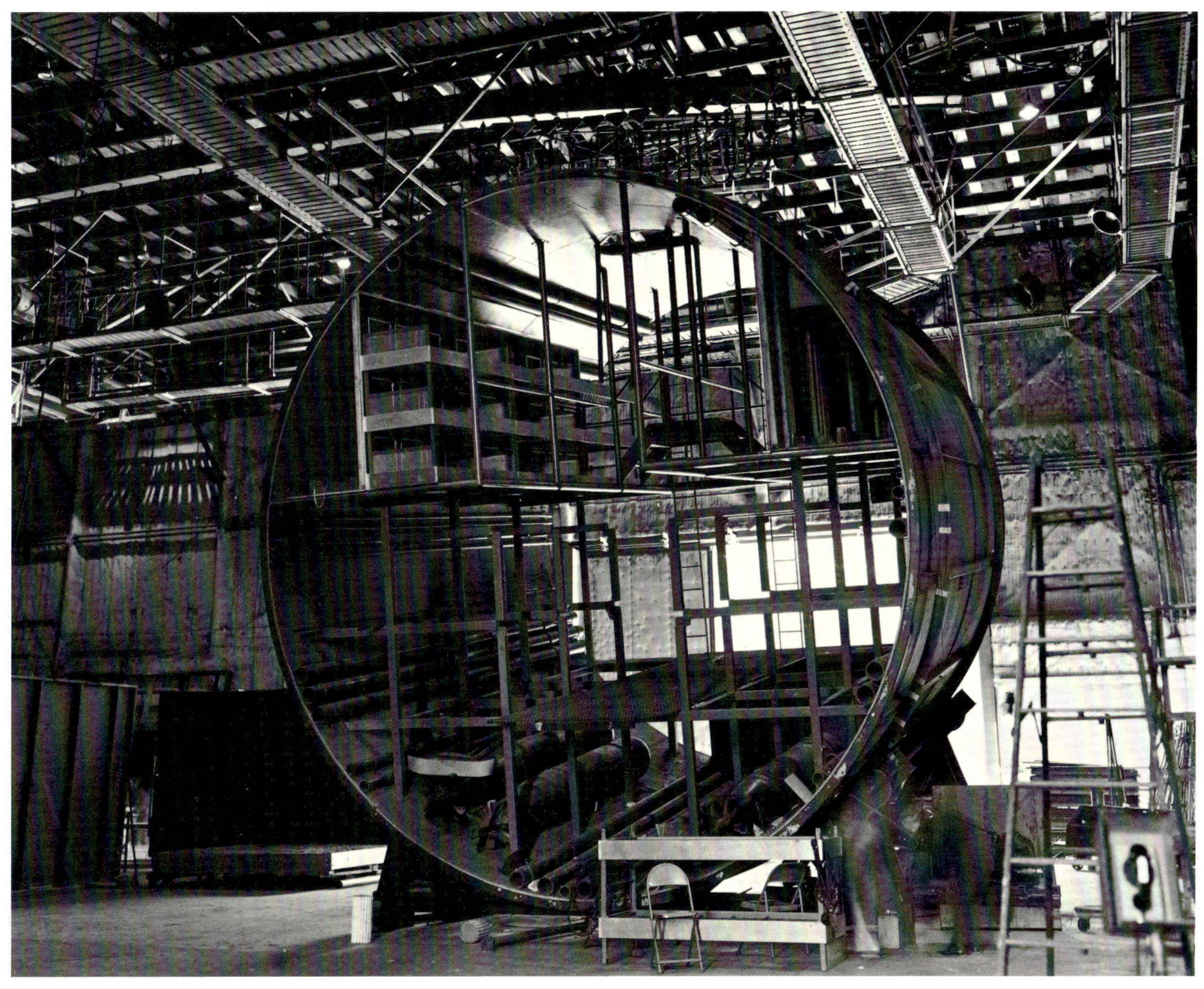

Plate 37: Submarine Cross-section; Feature Film, "Gray Lady Down", Stage #12, March 14, 1977

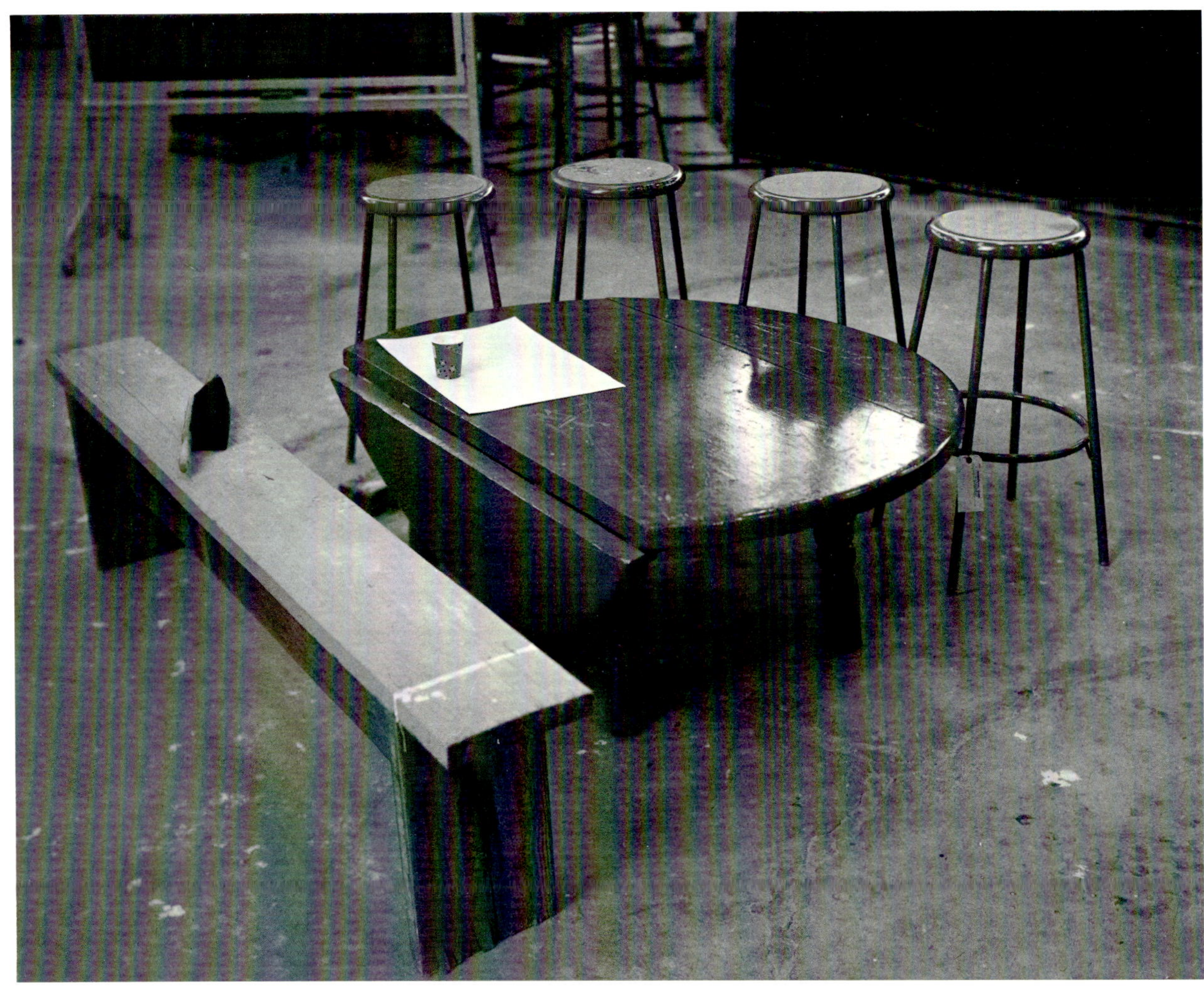

Plate 38: Accommodations About an Euclidean Table, 1978

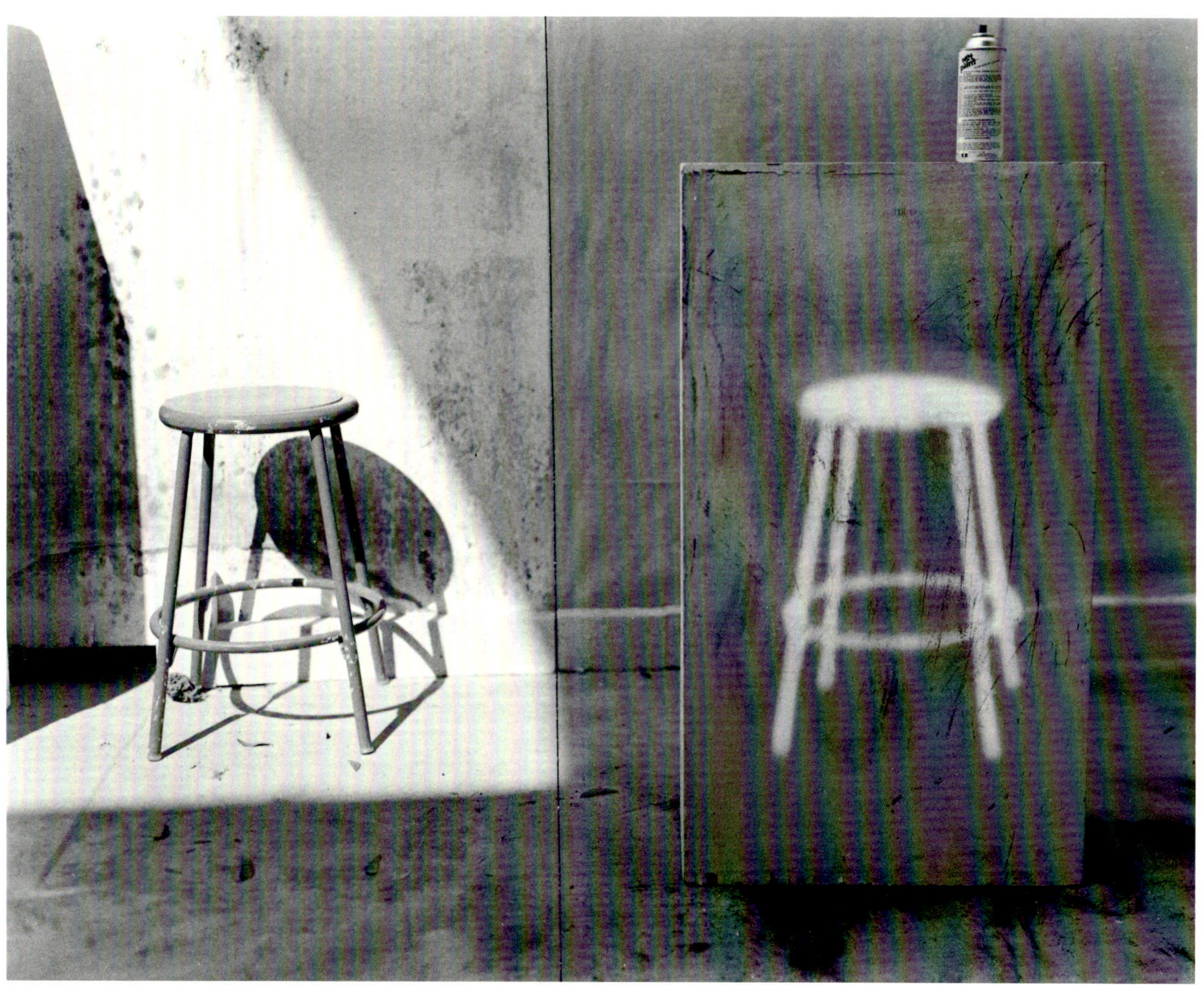

Plate 39: Quick Shift of the Head Leaves Glowing Stool Afterimage Posited on Pedestal, 1978

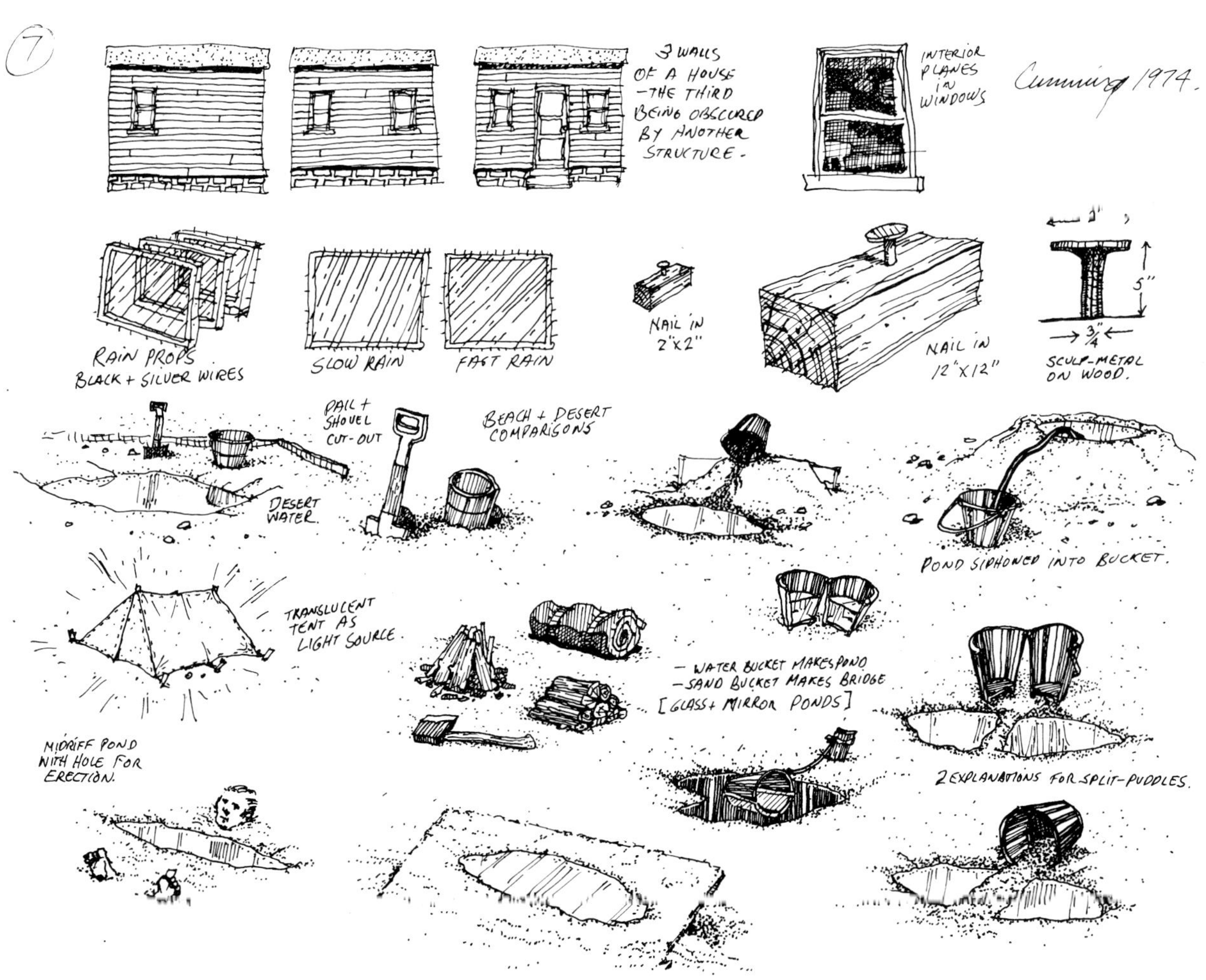

Drawing page #7, 1974

AN INTERVIEW WITH ROBERT CUMMING

Robert Cumming was born in Worcester, Massachusetts, on October 7, 1943. With the exception of an early year in Newfoundland, his first 20 years were spent in the greater Boston area, where he received an undergraduate degree in painting from the Massachusetts College of Art. Cumming went to graduate school at the University of Illinois from 1965 to 1967. His first teaching position was at the University of Wisconsin, Milwaukee, from 1967-1970. Cumming then moved to the greater Los Angeles area where he taught in the Art Department of California State University at Fullerton from 1970 to 1972, and later at several of the other local colleges. In 1978 he moved back to the East Coast to a position at the Hartford Art School. He currently lives in West Suffield, Connecticut.

Although Cumming's initial training was in painting, his art productions evolved with an overriding concern with sculpture and, finally, with photography. His preoccupations have always been conceptual, tinged with wit. He has received two National Endowment for the Arts grants and several other awards and commissions.

Five books of his photographs have been produced, primarily self-published. They are *Picture Fictions* (1971), *The Weight of Franchise Meat* (1971), *Training in the Arts* (1973), *Discourse on Domestic Disorder* (1975) and *Interruptions in Landscape and Logic* (1977). He has also published a portfolio of his photographs, taken at Universal Studios, titled *Studio Still Lifes* (1978).

His work has been exhibited in over 100 solo and group shows during the past decade. The museums which have his work in their permanent collections include the Museum of Modern Art, the Corcoran Gallery, the Museum of Fine Arts in Houston, the University of New Mexico, Pomona College and Cornell University.

In the following interview, which was made during the summer of 1978 in his studio, then in Orange, California, Cumming discusses the evolution of his art.

Let's start with your "training in the arts".
To a large extent I've taught myself in art. I have been a compulsive artist since I was in kindergarten. I was just drawing continuously.

Did your parents promote it?
As a kid I was pretty self-motivated, even stubborn, but my parents were always encouraging and never negative about the art work. After I got out of college they were there repeatedly during some very lean years. I went to high school in a little country town and I thought it was going to be really tough going to an art school in the big city. It wasn't. I went to the Massachusetts College of Art in Boston and majored in painting. After that I went to graduate school in the Art Department of the University of Illinois at Champaign-Urbana.

Was your major there painting?
Yes, it was a very odd situation. I had been accepted into the program as a painter because of my portfolio, but I was trying to find an exit from painting at that point. I was doing more constructions and 3-dimensional work, so in fact I wound up becoming a sculptor. I got a master's degree in painting none the less. I had a lot of trouble trying to pull that off. But what I was doing in sculpture wouldn't have been accepted by the sculpture department at Illinois anyway, so it was probably easier doing it in the "looser" painting department. There was also a very stiff set of requirements in printmaking, it was one of the sacred subjects at the University of Illinois. After two years of haggling with the department I got them to substitute photo credits so that I was majoring in painting but doing sculpture and minoring in printmaking but doing photography. The people I liked there were also doing or making similar adjustments. Bill Wegman was there at the same time. He was also into sculpture and process art and not necessarily painting on canvas.

Did you study photography with Art Sinsabaugh?
Yes, he was the instructor there. I was interested in doing montage work, probably something that looked like a Robert Rauschenberg piece. I certainly didn't want to do copperplate etching, which was their sacred printmaking medium. I wanted to do photo silkscreening and I thought photography would get me closer to it. I also needed to learn how to develop film and make prints and that sort of thing. Sinsabaugh was completely opposed to that type of photography, being

pretty much a purist. Our sensibilities were completely opposite. I admit to a certain amount of hard-headedness. I didn't want any of his large format photography and fine print quality at that point. It was useful information and I should have listened to him because it took a long time for me to learn that for myself later. I just saw Art a couple of weeks ago for the first time since then and we hit if off famously, but during the time of the student-teacher relationship it was different.

After receiving my MFA I taught for three years at the University of Wisconsin at Milwaukee.

Did you start doing photography more seriously while you were in Milwaukee?

Yes, once I got out of grad school I started doing more photography, though my primary interest was sculpture. I didn't know how to make anything so I set myself a goal to learn a different technique every year starting off with how to use plastics; and, for instance, I bought a sewing machine to learn how to sew. So each year I tried to learn a trade to reinforce my sculptures. I was into sculptures that looked very utilitarian and which had to incorporate a broad range of fabrication techniques. You have to know about 45 different types of screws to make a thing look convincing, to make it look like it was done out there in our industrialized society. So I learned how to use a #17 panhead screw with a lock washer rather than wood screw. The details had to be right.

You seem to be concerned with details in your photographs because you use an 8x10 view camera. Most artist/photographers who deal importantly with conceptual concerns in their work tend toward small format, with little concern for craftmanship. How did your use of an 8x10 come about?

Part of it was from being amazed by the details of 8x10 contact prints I had seen. I remember one photograph that affected me—it had a broad stretch of grass in the foreground, there was a little activity in the middle ground and a lot of sky. It was taken in Illinois out in all that flatness. I looked closer and closer and when I got way into it I realized it was a train track. There was a lot of confusion in this little quarter-inch strip of the print. It turned out to be a train wreck with maybe a couple of hundred people standing around the disaster scene. It really floored me that there was all of this information in this one little strip of the photograph. The reason you could see all the detail was because it was contact printed. I had been shooting 35mm and my work was very grainy. In fact, I found that the extreme grain was kind of an artsy turn on.

At that time, probably in 1965 before I left Boston, I picked up a copy of a book on Frederick Sommer and saw his Arizona landscapes. I was familiar with Aaron Siskind's photographs and I thought they were pretty compatible with what was going on in abstract expressionist painting, painters like Franz Kline. But there were Sommer's lancscapes done in the mid-40's that almost predicted what was to happen 20 years later—formalism and the flatness of the field for example. I was taken aback by the Arizona hillsides because I was just beginning to get involved in manic patterns, millions of little details. Sommer didn't seem to have a lot of that romantic overload which photography had in the 50's and even into the 60's. His work probably didn't influence me directly in terms of the pictures I took, but more in my thinking in making pictures, of what camera to use.

I started thinking about the whole view camera aesthetic after I got out of school. Originally I didn't want to go to anything as large as 8x10, but something larger than 4x5. I bought a 5x7 just to have; I thought I might photograph my sculpture. In eight months it was stolen. When I got the insurance money I bought an 8x10 and I have been using that camera ever since. It is a Burke and James body with a Schneider Symmar 300/500mm convertible lens.

In Milwaukee I started doing some straight photos with the 8x10. I was also documenting sculptures with it. These seemed to be two separate activities which later dovetailed and became almost one. Now I can't separate the two activities. I don't know sometimes whether I'm making sculpture and documenting it or building a prop for a photograph.

When you left Milwaukee in 1970 why did you choose Southern California?

I figured that as I got older it would be harder to make a radical jump to a new location. I was tired of the Midwest and wanted to move to one of the coasts. I was curious about all of the stuff I had seen in other photographs of California. Rather than go back East where everything

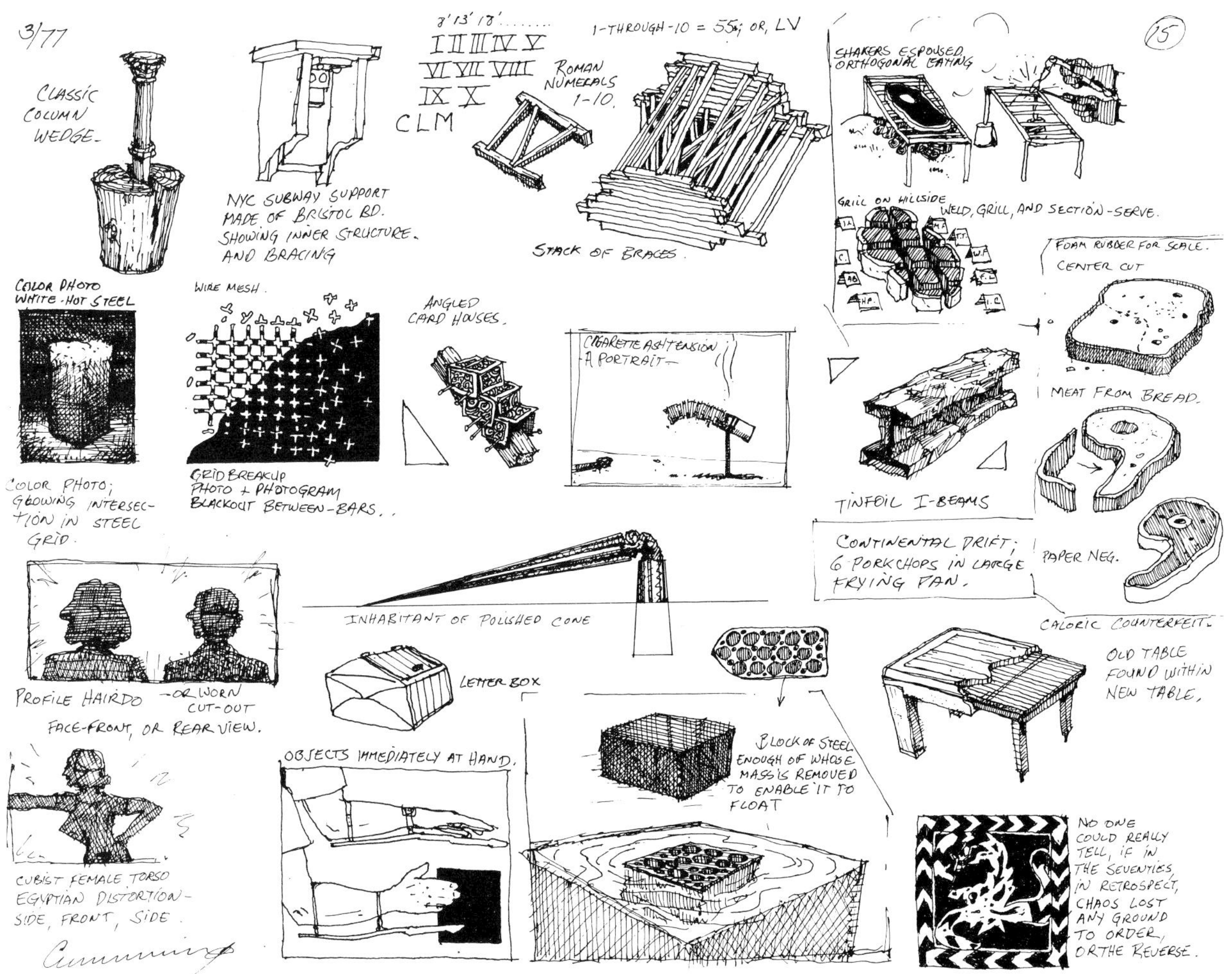

Drawing page #15, 1977

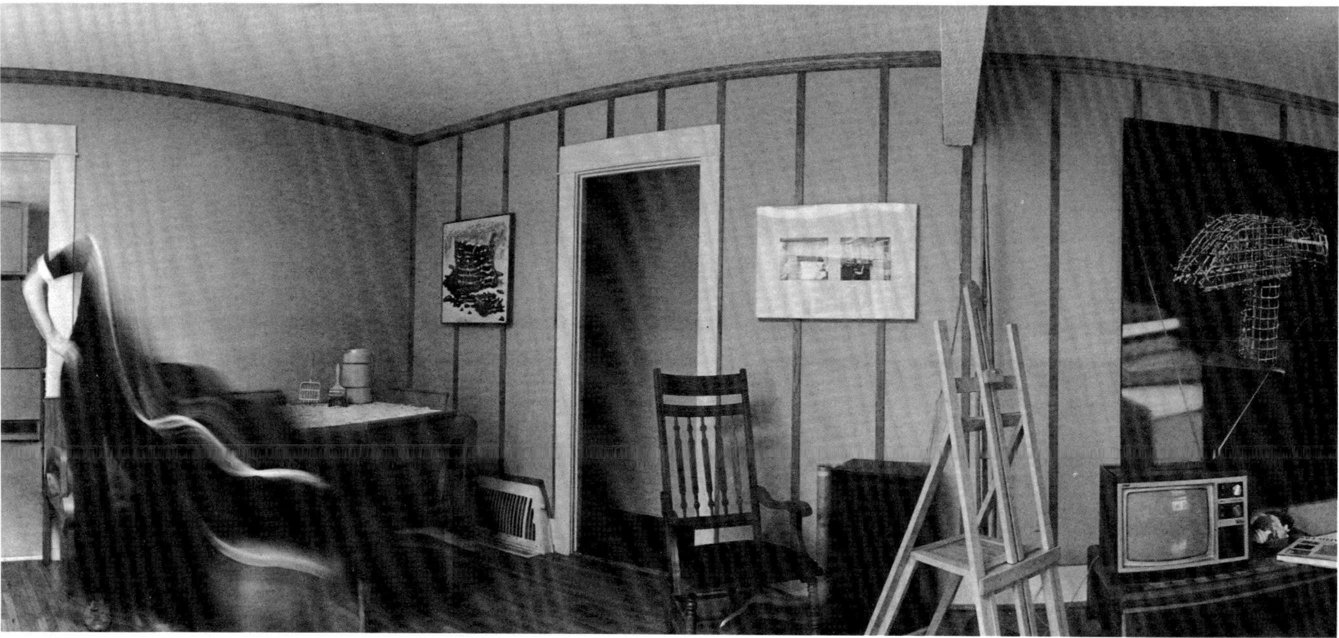

Cumming Going

Photograph by James Alinder, 1978

was comfy, where I had friends and family, I decided to opt for the other coast and see the rest of the country because I had never been west of the Mississippi. It might have been some of the Robert Frank pictures from *The Americans* that prompted that interest. Three of the Frank photographs dealt with Hollywood, two of a movie premier and one of a television studio. I thought they were just absolutely unreal. One is of a starlet out of focus, with this crowd of average-looking women who are behind the barriers looking at her, a public-to-celebrity relationship that I thought was really nice. Another Frank photo is of a television studio in Burbank. A woman is sitting on a stand in the studio. You can see her image on the screen, I think it is to the right of the picture, primarily from her shoulders to the top of her head. To the left hand side you can see the reality, with the woman sitting on a pretty rickety chair on top of this rolling plywood platform with miles of ugly black cable and this cheapo little decorative prop hanging down on fishing line. The reality and the television reality were so far apart. I think that was something I had to come to grips with after moving to California.

Were you exhibiting only sculpture at this time?
Sculpture and some photographs. Conceptual art, by that time, had arrived. Around 1969 you began to see some of the conceptual stuff by Burgy and Heubler, Kosuth, Dan Graham, Robert Barry and the others. I was beginning to latch on to that aspect of art with my picture taking. Somehow I was mixing conceptual concerns with the straight documentary things I was doing. I think my first book, *Picture Fictions,* mixes both of these tendencies. In 1973 I managed to get a gallery in New York to represent me. However, for some reason I wasn't showing at all in Los Angeles. It was only after recognition from the New York galleries that those in Los Angeles became interested in my work.

I think the photo world is a litttle more democratic and not as centralized as the art world. In the art world there is no such thing as having a little center in, for example, Albuquerque, New Mexico, where people are regularly shown in national photo exhibitions. There are these little pockets that manage to reinforce the photographic medium nationally, but it's not that way in the art world. There, it's much more closed, and more restricted to what comes out of New York. Eventually you have to deal with, if not live in, New York. The situation may have something to do with the portability of the medium. Photographs are highly portable. You just load them in

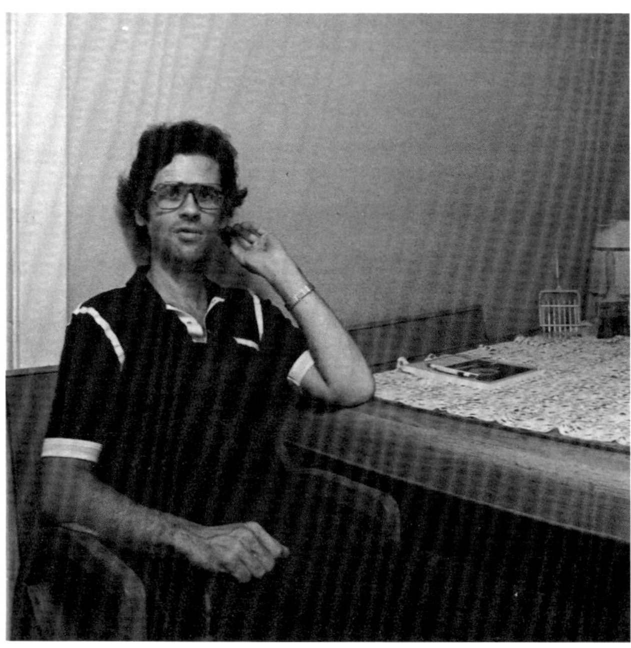

Robert Cumming

envelopes and off they go around the country, and if they are lost they can usually be reproduced.

Do you see the art world and the photography world as being separate worlds?
They have come a lot closer in the last couple of years. Many of the art galleries have opened up to photography. For example, in 1970 there would have been no way I could have gone to a gallery with a portfolio of photographs and presented them alongside my sculpture. They would have said, "What is this about? We only deal in sculpture." And the reverse was also true. I showed my early work to several photo galleries and they had trouble relating to my photographs and didn't understand my sculpture at all. To work in more than one area of art wasn't part of the dialogue back then. After these dismal early receptions, I pretty much decided to have nothing to do with the photo world, but to make photographs just because I liked them. And that's what I did for the next four or five years.

Have you formed many close friendships with other artists in the Los Angeles area?
In Los Angeles I have dealt very little with other artists. I've usually stayed pretty much to myself, but once a month or so I might go to an opening. I like to remain outside of the Los Angeles "art scene".

Why?
I don't know. I am really not sure. It doesn't seem to be something I really need. I value privacy a lot. It's really wierd—after admiring Frederick Sommer for those pictures back in 1965, I recently drove through Prescott, Arizona, where Sommer lives. I have heard that he is kind of a recluse and Prescott, Arizona, has got to be the town a recluse would choose to live in. It's almost inaccessable by car, a tiny little mining town. Anyway, I have always been somewhat reclusive. I don't seem to need a lot of interaction with other artists.

How were you first approached by people involved in photography in Los Angeles?
They did a show at Cal State Long Beach called *Photograph as Object, Photograph as Metaphor, Photograph as Document of a Concept.* John Upton was curating it and had selected Robert Heinecken and Minor White to fill two of the directions and needed a third person as a representative of newer conceptual ideas. John wasn't familiar with anyone working along those lines so Gene Cooper at Long Beach suggested he see my work. I think John felt he was being muscled into including me because at first he seemed disinterested in my pictures. About a week later he called and said, "I have been thinking about some of the things you said. I have been thinking about those pictures and would like to come back and talk to you again." He did, and after that became terribly enthusiastic about what the pictures represented. That was actually the first photo show I did. It was in 1973.

There was a mixed response from the Los Angeles photo community. At the opening I think most of the people had come to see Minor White, to a lesser extent Heinecken and not at all to see me. This was an entirely new audience for my work; I had been used to showing only to people who were interested in forms of conceptual art. While my photographs may be very pictorial for conceptual art, they are none the less conceptual. I was dealing with nicely resolved images, pictorial arrangements. I used a lot of backgrounds in photographs, while most conceptualists used blank backgrounds. I frequently placed situations in landscapes or with elaborate backgrounds and thought they were very pictorial all along, but the response to them was very strange. The audience was apparently trying to divine from them some of the existential mystery they found in the Minor White photographs. What I was doing basically was telling little stories, one and two part theatre pieces for objects. You read the first piece and then went on to the second piece, reading left to right. There was a dialogue presented in very straightforward narrative fashion and people suprisingly didn't see that. That was the first photography show, and after that I started getting invitations for more. Now I think more than half the shows I do are photography shows.

Working in several areas of art, how do you decide which to do at any given time?
It's all very random. I feel like doing one thing one day that gets involved in a project that might last two weeks to a month or maybe a year. I can't really plot it that rationally. I'm a little compulsive and very impatient. I may do something for two months and I get very tired of it and have to have a complete change. I'll do photographs for three months and then become incredibly restless with the lack of tactility of photographs and do something that may be the antithesis to it, like sculpture. Sculpture is very structural — making things fit, putting things together in almost a puzzle kind of fashion. It's more physical and tends to complement the other activity. I often switch back and forth between the two for the therapy alone. At one time the dual needs were splitting my work but now I seem to have found a way of compatibly incorporating the two opposing parts.

How are the concepts for your work developed and brought to realization?
In a number of ways. I'm fascinated with different phenomena and quirks in perception. I may see something happen in reality and then I'll elaborate on it.

Do you make lists?
No, it just sort of happens, it develops. I'll give you an example. I was going down the freeway one day behind a woman in a car who was driving rather slowly. As I watched her she was looking out the side window instead of looking ahead. And she kept looking out the side window going 55 mph, never glancing ahead. I had this terribly sick feeling in my stomach because at that speed you do need to glance ahead once in a while. So I had this momentary flash, this upset feeling, and I suddenly realized it was her hair on the left side of her head in a certain configuration that looked like a profile. Her hair had been combed in some arbitrary fashion so that from the side it looked like a nose and mouth. It was one of those split-second perceptual misreads that I noted as being quite extraordinary. When I came home I jotted it down and I did a couple of photographs based on that idea. My re-enactment involved cutting out profiles for people to wear on the sides of their heads.

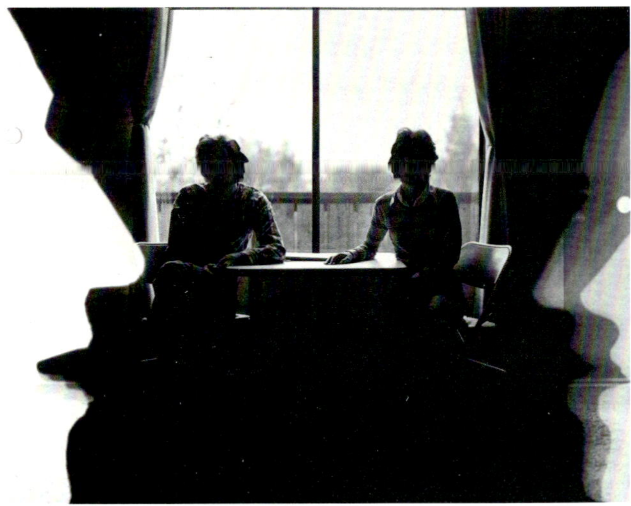

Couples in Profile, 1978

First comes the idea and then a sketch?
Yes, and even when I find something in nature quite often I'll sketch it instead of just writing it verbally. Some of the ideas, however, are just conceptualizations without any prompting from visual observation. I have spells when I get a flood of ideas and I make sketches of these because the execution may take awhile, especially if I have to build complex props.

Do you also consider your props as sculpture?
Yes, but I'm not always satisfied with the relationship between object and photo, the matter of documentation versus fabrication. Sometimes photographing these little perceptual situations is only a matter of rearranging an existing reality. For example, moving two or three chairs together in a room creates this kind of dialogue. And sometimes I just document a phenomenon as it exists in reality, so my work goes all the way from straight documentary transcription through a still-life kind of rearrangement to an entire rebuilding of nature.

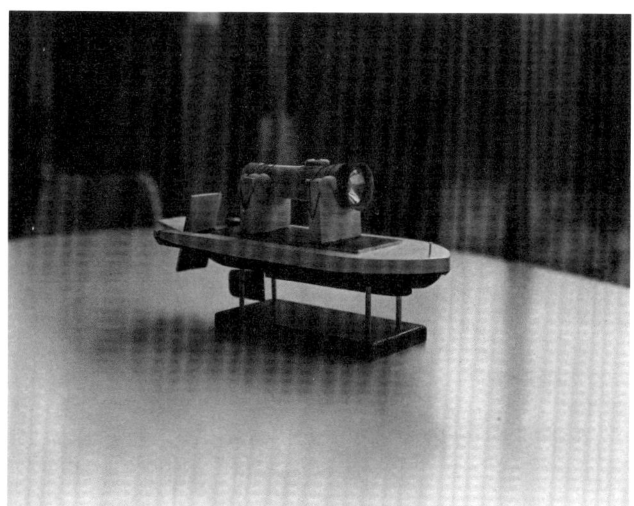

Light Boat Leaves Paths on Night Pool, 1975

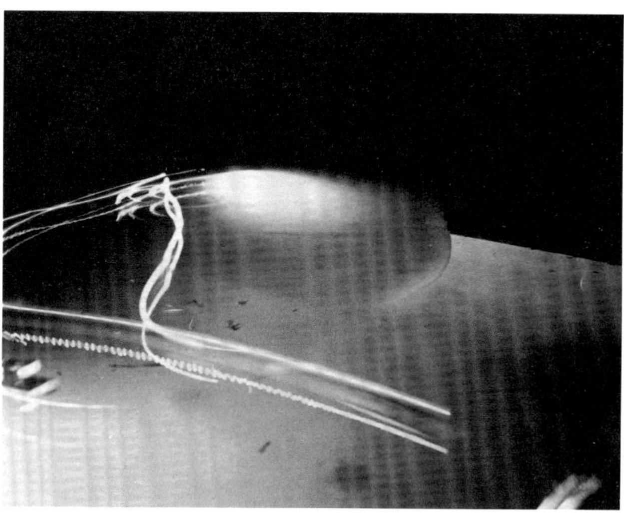

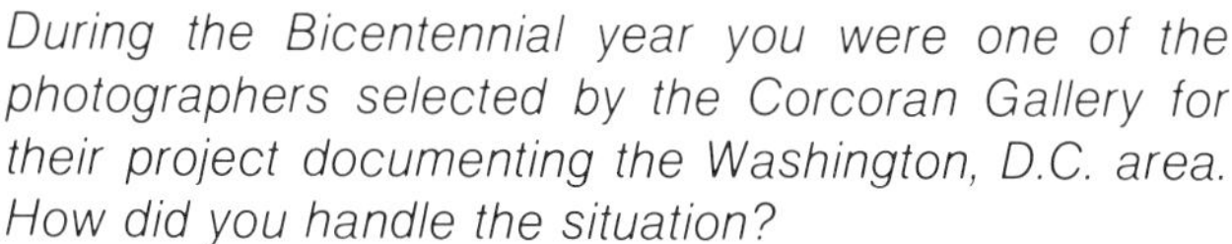

During the Bicentennial year you were one of the photographers selected by the Corcoran Gallery for their project documenting the Washington, D.C. area. How did you handle the situation?
I went to Washington for a month. I don't think I have worked as hard as that before, doing that many pieces in one month. There must have been 20 to 25 different pieces I did during the month, and that included all the prop-building as well as the photographs. I did the final printing back in Los Angeles. It was 16 hours a day for a month. It was very strenuous.

You recently completed a portfolio of photographs made in movie studios. It must have also taken a lot of energy.
Yes, it's the most strenuous thing over a long period of time I am sure I'll ever do. It was a phenomenal amount of work. I took 130 8x10 negatives over six months at Universal Studios, made over 2000 prints from these negatives and built 30 portfolio boxes. It took all of 1977. There must be 3000 hours of my life invested in that movie studio project.

During all of this time have you also been teaching?
Yes, it's necessary. I'm not to the point where I can make a living just from the sale of my work. Between teaching positions, for a while, I was a janitor. Then I worked in a sign shop for a year. Regarding my teaching, I'd ideally like to have a situation where I could teach a basic sculpture course, a photography course and a drawing course, rather than all of one. Art Departments, I've found, aren't that flexible.

Your photographs have often seemed to me to rely as much on wit as they do on concept. Can we talk about your sense of humor, your ideas about it?
Often things I do which I think of as serious, people find amusing. I don't like art that tells jokes. I hope my own work deals with wit and irony instead of simple joke-making. I like folk art, but I am too sophisticated to be a folk artist. It seems antithetical to me for artists to go through an extensive university training to develop a folk sensibility. It's too precocious. When I deal with humor in my photographs I think I am partly laughing at the quirks of my own mind. I tend to over-describe things and to make everything overly logical.

Is it overly logical to attach a flash-light to a piece of wood, add a rubber-band-powered motor and run it around the swimming pool?
Now that's absurd.

And add to this an earlier image of a slice of bread imbedded in the side of a watermelon.
I guess that would just be ironic. It's hard for me to analyze that part of my work. One of the things that is absurd about my photographs is the proportion of work involved, in other words, why would anyone reconstruct this entire reality for such small gain? Why build 100

mosquitoes? Why? Because I wanted to take a photograph where they are all evenly distributed. There is kind of an imbalance between the initial idea and the eventual execution. There are parallels. I've always like the dioramas in the natural history museums. Some are of relatively insignificant moments, like a trout jumping out of a pond to eat a mosquito, but the museum has presented this beautiful illusionistic pond with a scenic background and the trout magically hanging in the air above the water. To me that seems an equally illogical application of time and energy.

I think my photographs have been growing progressively less humorous. I have been trying to purge the obvious humor from them. Some of the early ones were intended to be outright gut-busters. Around 1970 I did photographs I referred to as visual one-liners. I think the later pictures are more involved. They are more complicated and work on more levels.

How do your titles come about and how important are they to understanding the work?
I think they are partly a key to interpretation. They focus on certain things, certain actions which are happening in the picture. They seem to give you my reason for taking them. In some cases captions are really necessary for the viewer to understand what I think the photo is about. Yet there are some photos which are purely visual, where I add the title as a smoke screen. The wording is really important, yet I try to keep the words to a minimum. I have been experimenting with putting the captions directly on the negative. The titles are the same but they are incorporated into the photograph. It makes the picture more complex but sometimes it's broken my heart to add words on top of the print. I'll know if it's going to work after doing a few more pieces. With the Studio Still Lifes portfolio prints all the captions are superimposed photographically beneath the photos.

How many photographic pieces do you do a year?
I think on the order of 30.

Do they come in batches or at regular intervals?
I usually find myself getting exuberant and I do a whole bunch and print like crazy.

Now you see yourself doing more single images?
Yes, I have been going back through a lot of catalogues from museum shows and I decided a lot of pictures look better by themselves; just one picture, not a group.

What is the longest time you have spent preparing for and making a single photograph?
Including the building of a prop, about 3 months.

You have in part built your reputation through a series of books in which photography has played a central role. I'm curious as to how that began and also about the use of words and pictures in the later books.
After doing the first one, *Picture Fictions,* I thought bookmaking was fantastic. I said, "I am going to do this for the rest of my life — put pictures in books and send them out. It's going to make me a lot of money and I won't have to teach any more, do odd jobs or that sort of thing." I did another book in 1971 called *The Weight of Franchise Meat.* The idea was to go to all the fast-food hamburger places and actually weigh the burgers and give the results in words and pictures, accurately reported in the book. I conceived it as being about sixteen pictures, and took them in about two days. I don't think it had the depth of *Picture Fictions* or the other books. *Picture Fictions* was a selection of photographs from three years work. *Franchise Meat* was the result of acting prematurely on a very obvious idea.

I thought the concept was valuable in 1971.
It's too California and a little too easy. I did it right after I arrived in Los Angeles, I was really thrilled about a lot of things about California. The hamburger was one of the things I wanted to spot-light. The book turned out thin and I have tried to hide it.

Did you actually eat the hamburgers?
Yes, sixteen hamburgers in two days. I got this incredible case of dysentery, the sickest I can ever remember.

Your three most recent books, Training in the Arts, Discourse on Domestic Disorder *and* Interruptions in Landscape and Logic *you see as a trilogy.*
Right now, I'm most interested in the trilogy, for the way in which it handles the combinations of photos and text. The narrative element is a traditionally developed short-story form. These books are experiments in an unfamiliar medium. They test the possibilities of a form that allows a deeper layering of meanings than is possible with single or double static pictures.

Though the visual design of the trilogy makes the books look alike, they exercise three different forms of story exposition; tongue-in-cheek satire, boredom and inconsequential story-telling and a darker experiment with the forces of destruction in war.

What projects do you have coming up?
I have been doing a series of eight paintings, huge colorful pictures 6x8 feet just for a change. I had thought it would take me only two or three days per painting, but they have ended up taking a month each. I have only done three and a half. I have one project which scares the shit out of me because it is so involved and so big. I am thinking of writing a short novel. I think it would take about 10 years to do, but I'm fed up with projects.

Why, after eight years here in Southern California, are you moving back east now?
I think I came to California out of curiosity and that curiosity has been pretty well satisfied. I find myself changing. Doing the *Studio Still Life Portfolio* felt like driving the last nail in the coffin in terms of using up what I could get from Southern California. It is not only using up ideas, but my enthusiasm for the fakery and illusionism of Hollywood has been depleted. I think the illusionistic photographs are instructive in terms of the ethics of illusion. I was dealing so successfully with illusion that I could have made people think what they were looking at was reality. But that would have been out and out deception, which is not what I am interested in. I'm interested in causing people to catch themselves misreading the photographs.

Have you begun to reflect on the experience of California in your work?
The California environment has had a big influence on my work. Now I am curious about what effect going back east will have on me. There is a different landscape and different people.